SUSTAINED BY
JOY

SUSTAINED BY JOY

STUDIES IN PHILIPPIANS
GEORGE B. DUNCAN

Pickering & Inglis
LONDON · GLASGOW

ISBN 0 7208 0469 8
Cat. No. 01/1835

Most of the material in this book
was previously issued under the title

The Life of Continual Rejoicing

To My Wife

CONTENTS

		PAGE
1 THE CHURCH AT PHILIPPI	1:1–11	11
2 JOY – AND THE PLACE I'M IN	1:12–26	35
3 JOY – AND THE PEOPLE I'M WITH	1:27–2.30	57
4 JOY – AND THE PERSON I AM	3:1–21	81
5 THE CONCLUSION OF THE LETTER	4:1–23	105

INTRODUCTORY NOTE

I HAVE NEVER FELT that the giving of Bible Readings at Conventions has been my particular gift, but I was urged to undertake this ministry at Filey in 1960. These addresses, recorded at the time, were given in the two ballrooms in which the holiday campers met each morning. Their purpose was not so much to give a word by word, or verse by verse, exposition of this wonderful epistle, but rather to extract the main lessons in the letter and relate them to the everyday life of ordinary folk.

Like all other preachers, I owe a great debt to others who have sought to expound the truths set out here, but I owe still more to those who prayed for the Bible Readings and the one who was to give them. I shall long retain the memory of those two hours each morning when the Bible Reading was given first in the Viennese Ballroom to one half of the camp, and then, after the hurried journey to the Regency Ballroom, to the other half. I felt that God undertook for me in the ministry, morning by morning, and that the close attention of those great audiences indicated that the Lord was blessing the spoken word.

At that time, Mr A. Lindsay Glegg, President of the Movement for World Evangelisation, very kindly wrote that 'The Bible Readings were so greatly appreciated that many desired to have a more permanent record ... It is hoped that in cold print these messages will still retain much of their warm spiritual impact and power, so manifest at the time of their delivery.'

May the same Lord who graciously used the spoken message then, be pleased to bless to many more the written version of these studies.

G. B. Duncan

PAUL and Timotheus, the servants of Jesus Christ, to all the saints in Christ Jesus which are at Philippi, with the bishops and deacons:

2 Grace *be* unto you, and peace, from God our Father, and *from* the Lord Jesus Christ.

3 I thank my God upon every remembrance of you.

4 Always in every prayer of mine for you all making request with joy.

5 For your fellowship in the gospel from the first day until now;

6 Being confident of this very thing, that he which hath begun a good work in you will perform *it* until the day of Jesus Christ:

7 Even as it is meet for me to think this of you all, because I have you in my heart; inasmuch as both in my bonds, and in the defence and confirmation of the gospel, ye all are partakers of my grace.

8 For God is my record, how greatly I long after you all in the bowels of Jesus Christ.

9 And this I pray, that your love may abound yet more and more in knowledge and *in* all judgment;

10 That ye may approve things that are excellent; that ye may be sincere and without offence till the day of Christ;

11 Being filled with the fruits of righteousness, which are by Jesus Christ, unto the glory and praise of God.

1

THE CHURCH AT PHILIPPI

THE LETTER OF Paul to the Philippians
has been called 'The Epistle of Joy' and
when we come to it, we find that it
contains very little in the way of fault-finding.
That may be refreshing for us because my
experience in the ministry – both in the average
church pulpit and in the usual convention – is
that the congregation comes in for a good deal of
rough treatment. We all of us know what it is to
go out from a service feeling we have just been
flogged!

Here is one epistle at any rate where, if there
is any fault-finding, it will be by reflection
rather than by direct statement. There is almost
nothing in the way of censure that Paul has to
utter in this wonderfully intimate and
affectionate letter. He is writing from Rome,
where he is in bonds and a prisoner, to the
Church at Philippi in Macedonia.

The main theme in our study is that of

REJOICING; the theme which appears constantly throughout this epistle. By way of introduction I would like to recapture a phrase from a memory of the Keswick Convention many years ago when I heard Bishop Taylor Smith preaching in St. John's Church. Although I have forgotten everything else he said – that happens to sermons, I'm afraid: they are mostly forgotten, except for the odd phrase or the odd sentence – one phrase he used that Sunday has stayed in my memory ever since. He said that the Christian was meant to live 'a life of continual rejoicing'!

That seems a very hard statement to make but when we read this epistle through, with its constant undercurrent of harmony and joy and praise, we get an inkling of the way we too can live such a life. We do well to remember that the Christian life is meant to be a radiant and a rejoicing life. The second named part of the wonderful cluster of the fruit of the Spirit described by Paul is JOY, and the mark of a really fully-balanced and fully-lived Christian life is that it is a joyous experience. We ought to be a joyful people!

First we must notice the epistle's striking introduction: in subsequent studies we will get on to our main theme of the Life of Continual Rejoicing.

The introduction lies in the first eleven verses of this first chapter and this section may be regarded as the avenue up to the big house. It is an avenue in which there are many lessons to learn and things to notice.

Let us note the three-fold division of these eleven verses. Verses 1 and 2 contain obviously the greeting that Paul is sending to all the saints in Christ Jesus which are at Philippi. Then in verses 3–8, the theme changes slightly, beginning with the words 'I thank my God': that gives us the emphasis in these verses. The key verse in this section is verse 5 '... I thank my God ... for your fellowship in the gospel from the first day until now.' Here is stated the gratitude that he would show. And then in the final section commencing at verse 9, he turns to prayer. Having been thankful for so much, he is still not satisfied, but goes on (vv. 9–11) '... and this I pray, that your love may abound yet more and more ...' *The greeting he sends – the gratitude he shows –* and *the growth he seeks.* That seems to me a very logical and inevitable division of the opening introduction to this epistle.

Review the words again, carrying in mind these three thoughts – *the greeting sent, the gratitude shown,* and *the growth sought.* 'Paul and Timothy ... to all the saints in Christ Jesus which are at Philippi ... Grace be unto you and peace ... I thank my God upon every remembrance of you ... for your fellowship in the gospel from the first day until now; being confident of this very thing, that he which hath begun a good work in you will perform it until the day of Jesus Christ ... And this I pray, that your love may abound yet more and more in knowledge and in all judgment; that ye may approve things that are excellent; that ye may be

sincere and without offence till the day of
Christ; being filled with the fruits of
righteousness which are by Jesus Christ, unto
the glory and praise of God.'

1. THE GREETING HE SENDS (vv. 1, 2)

We must probe down behind these titles,
these divisions, in order to learn some of the
timeless truths which lie hidden within this
particular passage. So, to study the first two
verses, *The greeting sent*, probe behind the mere
greeting and discover how it was that this
Church at Philippi came into being at all.

It is described in the opening verse as
consisting of 'all the saints in Christ Jesus which
are at Philippi'. Let us then turn back to Acts
16, verses 7 to the end, where we can study the
birth of this church. How did it all begin? How
does any church begin? How does any spiritual
work come into existence? The story in Acts 16
is familiar; we all remember that this was the
first church founded in Europe. Paul had
travelled widely in Asia Minor, and then was
called over to Macedonia and so came to
Philippi. It was not only the first church in
Europe, but its building was marked by some
very wonderful conversions, some of which are
recorded in Luke's chapter. There was Lydia's
conversion; that of the demented and devil-
possessed slave girl; and there was the shattering
experience of the keeper of the jail – you will
remember the story. But what lay underneath
and behind all this? What are the principles

upon which any work of God depends and is built?

First of all, in Acts 17: 7–10, we find that the primary requisite in the establishing of any spiritual work for God is

(i) *The Obedience of the Servant*

It is significant that everything turned upon Paul's obedience; whether there was to be a church at Philippi at all depended on that. And the obedience was two-fold in character. First of all, God closed a door. 'After they were come to Mysia, they assayed to go into Bithynia: but the Spirit suffered them not' (Acts 16: 7). That is to say, God said to Paul and Silas, there is something you are *not* to do. And Paul accepted the closure of that door.

But with the closing of one door, another door opened. A vision appeared to Paul in the night. 'There stood a man of Macedonia, and prayed him, saying, "Come over into Macedonia, and help us." And after he had seen the vision, immediately we endeavoured to go into Macedonia, assuredly gathering that the Lord had called us for to preach the gospel unto them.' *The obedience of the servant*.

Is there not something to be learned from this? Are we not suffering, in evangelical circles, from over-familiarity with the truth of the forgiveness of sins? We have almost come to think it doesn't really matter whether we obey God or not – it doesn't matter if I do something God has said I am not to do: or if I don't do something God has told me to do, because I can

simply turn to 1 John 1 and claim the promise
'If we confess our sins, God is faithful and just
to forgive us our sins and to cleanse us from all
unrighteousness'. We are in serious danger of
taking up the attitude which says – 'It doesn't
matter if I sin'.

One lesson that stands out vividly in this
particular passage is that the *work* of God
depends upon the *men* of God and ultimately
upon *obedience* to God. It matters profoundly if
you and I are disobedient to the will of God.
Indeed I think we can say that in evangelical
Christendom today, the whole issue that God
has with the church does not lie in the realm of
ignorance – already we *know* so much; it is our
obedience that is at fault, we fail to *do* the will
of God.

Was it Finney who said that revival consists
simply in a new obedience? If you and I were
merely to go out and do all that we know
perfectly well God means us to do, revival
would break out tomorrow! So here we find that
the very existence of a church depends upon the
obedience of one man, one prepared to accept
God's forbidding and prepared to obey God's
calling. I sometimes wonder what the situation
would be in our land today – indeed in every
land which the church of Jesus Christ has
already reached – if God could only find men
and women prepared to do exactly what he
asked. *The obedience of a servant* – the whole
situation at Philippi turned on that.

How much does the situation in your hospital,
your church, your school, your business, your

factory, your shop, your home, turn upon your obedience? *The obedience of the servant*: that is the first thing that contributed to this church: its very existence had turned upon his own obedience. Even so, there may be people that God is wanting to reach and he cannot contact them because he cannot get to them through you.

The second thing that marked the birth of this church was

(ii) *The Operation of the Spirit*

Right at the heart of the birth of this church lay the miracle of regeneration, of conversion. I am glad that in this particular church we have been given a wide range both of the *types* of people who were converted and of the *ways* in which conversion came to them.

First of all there was Lydia – a wealthy business-woman, successful, and deeply religious. Then there was the devil-possessed slave girl, utterly degraded, quite probably a woman of the streets. There was a civil servant, a government official, in charge of the prison, a man conscientiously thorough in all that he did. These were the types.

And how varied was the experience of conversion that they received! Lydia was converted quietly. Indeed hers is possibly the loveliest conversion anywhere in the New Testament. 'Lydia, whose heart the Lord opened.' Is somebody reading this who is a little bit frightened of 'being converted' because you feel that it is a noisy, emotional experience? I

doubt if God cares very much *how* you are
converted: what does concern God is the fact
that you must be converted; that you are born
again of the Spirit of God; that you have opened
your personality to the incoming of Christ by
the Holy Spirit; that you possess the New Life
in Christ.

This woman, Lydia, was deeply religious, and
she was converted at church. Are *you* deeply
religious, yet not converted? Are you a person of
culture, of wealth, of business success, a church
member? Maybe, but are you *converted*? That is
the question. Have you been born again? Jesus
said to a religious leader of his day, 'Except a
man be born again, he cannot enter the
kingdom.' He cannot even see it.

Some people are converted quietly like Lydia,
a lovely conversion – 'Lydia, whose heart the
Lord opened'. Others are converted
dramatically, like the keeper of the prison, in a
veritable earthquake of emotion. They are
broken down. Their whole world seems to rock.
They are swept with tears and repentance; then
they spring to their feet in faith and surrender
and song. Some people are converted like that. I
wasn't, but some are.

Some are converted quietly, some
dramatically, but others are converted very
wonderfully from the very depths of utter,
hopeless degradation. It is possible that someone
reading these lines may feel that he – or she –
has passed beyond the converting power and
grace of God. You know that your heart and life
for years have been so stained with sin that you

wonder why you should have come across these words. God only knows. You have certainly already made up your mind that you can never become a Christian; you have gone too far, too deeply into sin, it's been delayed too long! But some people are converted very wonderfully from the depths of utter and hopeless degradation, like this demon-possessed girl at Philippi. Nothing is beyond the grace and power of Jesus Christ, and *the operation of the Spirit*.

One of the tragedies of so much church life today is that we have church members who are not members of Christ! One of the ancient fathers put the definition of the church in simple but lovely language: 'Where Christ is, there is the church.' That condenses the whole truth in a nutshell. Not 'where a membership roll is', not 'where the sacraments are', not even 'where the ministry of the Word is', but *'where Christ is, there is the church'*.

That is the language of the New Testament. It is the language of John the Apostle when he writes in his first epistle 'He that hath the Son hath life. He that hath not the Son hath not life' (5: 12). Without *the operation of the Spirit* there could be no church.

And there was a third factor in the birth of this church:

(iii) *The Opposition of Society*

It is worth remembering that Christianity is seldom popular when God is really working. Here at Philippi opposition was immediately aroused; financial interests were involved. Paul

and Silas were thrown into prison after being
flogged with many stripes. There is always
travail when the church is born. I think one of
the sad things about us modern Christians is
that we expect the Spirit of God to work
without cost, without *pain*. *There are always
birth-pangs*. These men had bleeding backs as
others were being born again. It was 'to all the
saints in Christ Jesus which are at Philippi', a
church born out of suffering, that Paul sent
greetings.

Returning now from Acts 16 to Philippians
1:3–8, move on from the GREETING Paul sent to –

2. THE GRATITUDE HE SHOWS (vv. 3–8)

'I thank my God upon every remembrance of
you' (v. 3). When I read the words 'I thank'
I ask myself, is gratitude one of the graces we
are losing today? I think we are living in days
when there is a very real tendency to take
everything for granted. The welfare state is
contributing to this attitude; but it is spreading
into the church, until evangelical Christians are
beginning to take the grace of God for granted.

'I thank': when did *you* last give thanks to
God? How many churches have ever had a Praise
Meeting? Some have *Prayer* Meetings – and
some do not. (I am always sorry for a church
that has no prayer meeting; if it has no prayer it
will have no blessing.) But how many churches
that do have prayer meetings ever stop to give
thanks to God?

Is not gratitude a lovely thing? Do you not

feel hurt when you give a lovely gift to somebody, if he never stops to say thank you? I wonder how many times God is deeply hurt by our lack of gratitude. Are we ever grateful enough, not only to God, but also to other members of the church? Paul's depth of character is revealed here, by *the gratitude he shows*. This is the first thing that he is doing, being grateful.

Do you remember when our Lord healed ten lepers, and only one came back? Our Lord said, 'Were there not ten cleansed, and where are the nine? Is there but one that has returned to give thanks?' Only one grateful – I think we all need to cultivate the spirit of gratitude in our relationships, remembering to say 'thank you' when others are waiting upon us, serving us. Occasionally, even at Christian Conferences, those at the controlling end of things are hurt and ashamed when they receive the odd report, spoken kindly but faithfully, that some supposedly Christian people have not been nice to the staff. That is tragic in a Christian community! Be grateful, be nice, be kind. I remember the man in charge of one camp, after his first experience of a Christian Crusade, rising at the Farewell Meeting to testify, 'All through this week my staff have been saying "These people must have something because they are so nice".' Well, be nice and be grateful. What a difference it makes to be thanked, to feel that we are appreciated!

But what is Paul thanking the Philippians for? He is grateful 'for their fellowship in the

furtherance of the gospel from the first day
until now' (v. 5). That is to say, the thing that
he is deeply thankful for is their fellowship. And
so, having looked at the birth of the church, let
us consider next *the bonds of the church's
fellowship*.

There is a wonderful bond between Christian
and Christian, and three strands that comprise
it. They are all brought out in verses 3–8, so
warm with affection and intimate in their
references. The first bond in fellowship is

(i) *A life common to the fellowship*

Look at verse 7, the final phrase. Here the
true rendering is not 'ye are all partakers of my
grace', but rather, 'ye are all partakers with me of
grace'. That is to say, Paul was writing to a
fellowship in which he rejoiced, for which he
was grateful, which had at its very heart a life
common to the fellowship, one in which he himself shared. 'Ye are all partakers with me of grace.'

Now this is a profound truth and a very
wonderful one, that Christians are partakers
of the same life. Lydia, the wealthy business-
woman, did not receive a special grade of
spiritual life, suited to her high social standing
and different from the life given to the
degraded, demented, devil-possessed slave girl,
who would get a kind of inferior quality suited
to her social status! Nor did the civil servant get
a different kind suited to him! The Christ they
received was the same, the one Christ. And if
the colour of a man's skin is yellow or brown,
the Christ he receives is the same Christ whom

you receive and I receive, whose skins are white.

Let us hold on to this. It is a wonderful fact of experience, a glorious truth. I remember Professor Blaiklock bearing testimony to it at Keswick. Setting out from Auckland University on his Sabbatical Year, he said how he thanked God for Christian fellowship, and how sorry he felt for colleagues who were not Christians setting out on a similar world tour. He explained: 'You see, wherever I travel I have friends. Wherever they go they meet strangers: I meet other members of the family.'

In my own world travels it was perfectly wonderful to experience this fellowship. I would go to Australia, New Zealand, Honolulu, the States, South Africa, Rhodesia, Kenya, Uganda, Japan, South America it did not matter *where* I went; *there* I would be introduced to some Christian, a stranger to me but born again of the Spirit of God. Within five minutes we would feel as if we had known each other for years! Why? Because of *the life common to the fellowship*.

Differences do not matter, basically, whether they be of educational background or social standing. There is no such thing as snobbery within the Christian church. I cannot be snobbish about my Christ and look down on you, indwelt by the same Christ! Neither can you look down on me or on my Christ! It would be impertinence and blasphemy. The one bond that binds together is Christ.

I wonder if this explains why some people feel out of the fellowship. Are you a member of a

lively church where there is a fine group of keen
people? Are you in a hospital where there is a
group of keen nurses? And you feel right out of
it! They do not appear to talk your language.
You are ill at ease in their company; you feel a
stranger. Do you wonder why this should be? I
think I know why: you are not in the fellowship.
Do you know why you are not in the fellowship?
Because you have not the life shared by the
fellowship. You have never received Christ.
There is no bond. Receive Christ and you
receive the *life common to the fellowship* – and
you are right in!

I find also here

(ii) *A love constraining in the fellowship*

Look at verse 7: right in the centre we read 'I
have you in my heart'. Then in verse 8 'God is
my witness how greatly I long after you with the
very love of Jesus Christ.' That is the real
significance of the words. 'The very love of
Christ' is motivating my whole relationship with
you, governing my whole attitude towards you –
love constraining in the fellowship.

What is the explanation of this? It is very
simple. When you receive the life of Christ, you
receive the love of Christ. You cannot separate
his life from his love. Every one of us must have
known this experimentally. Do you remember
how, before you were converted, you were never
particularly interested in the church, and you
very seldom attended? You were not interested
in the Bible – you hardly ever read it. As for
Christian people, you just hoped you'd never be

associated with that bunch of peculiar, odd sort of folk that you despised, and by whom you were always embarrassed! But *after* you were converted, you found that you were drawn to the Word of God. You began to love it. You found that you couldn't keep away from the living church – and so you went. And as for the peculiar group of folk that you had always been embarrassed by, with whom you felt uncomfortable, now you have found your greatest friends among them.

What had happened? Well, not only had a new *life* come in, but a new *love*. That is what Paul talks about in Romans 5:5 'The love of God is shed abroad in our hearts by the Holy Ghost which is given to us.'

Notice, too, how constantly Love thinks of those loved: 'I thank my God upon *every remembrance* of you.' Paul could never calculate how often he thought of the Philippian Christians and prayed for them. But then, how constantly Love does think of those loved. Are any mothers or fathers reading this, whose child is absent – for the first time maybe? Tell me this, you have been thinking of them, haven't you, constantly, wondering how they are getting on? Is there a husband skimming these lines, distant from his wife? Or someone who has had to leave a loved one unexpectedly in hospital – you are thinking of that one, all the time as you read.

Do you, in your fellowship in your church, think like *that* of one another? 'I thank my God upon *every* remembrance of you.' How

constantly Love thinks of those loved – and how
intimately. Paul says 'I have you in my heart.'
Everywhere I go, I carry you around with me,
thinking of you – your needs, your successes,
your work. What a wonderful love was this! Is
there a fellow sharing these studies who is
engaged to be married? There is a girl you love.
She promised to be your wife and you have
promised to marry her. What have you in your
pocket book right now. I can tell you – you have
a photograph of her. And you carry that around
with you always. Is a husband reading this? You
have a pocket book too, and a photograph! Oh,
it may have been taken a long time ago, and if
you took it out now you would hardly recognize
the girl you married! But anyway, she is there.
That's what she looked like until you started
dealing with her!

'I have you in my heart.' If only we could get
this warmth of fellowship into the church today,
what a difference it would make. 'I have you in
my heart ... every remembrance of you.' What
affection and love there was in this wonderful
group, between Paul and themselves and
between themselves and Paul. What a difference
there would be in every church or mission if it
was like this.

Is there anything more to note about this
love? It was mindful – we've thought of that. It
was grateful – we have thought of that. There is
something further here suggested by the phrase
'Your fellowship ... in the furtherance of the
gospel, *from the first day until now*'. That
covered a span of approximately ten years. Paul

was grateful for their fellowship in the
furtherance of the gospel over a span of ten
years. Well, if he is grateful for it over such a
long period of time, I think we can be quite
certain of one more thing about that fellowship.
It must have been absolutely dependable and
reliable. Here was a fellowship, here was a
relationship, between Christians that had been
tested out, and Paul is grateful for it, because it
was so reliable!

I wonder are people grateful for your
fellowship because it is reliable, and dependable,
and wonderful? Or are people just fed up with
your unreliability? We seem to be living in days
when dependability, reliability, responsibility,
are almost forgotten features of life. I gather it is
so in industry. Can your boss depend on you?
Is he grateful for you? Is he glad that he has
you as a secretary? Your Sunday School
Superintendent – is he very grateful that you're
in the fellowship with him for the furtherance of
the gospel among the children? Are you so
reliable, so dependable, so faithful that he
thanks God on every remembrance of you? Is
your minister grateful for you? Does he know
that you're going to be at the prayer meeting
come rain, come wind? Is he thankful that
you're one of his flock? – grateful for your
fellowship in the furtherance of the gospel from
the first day until now?

Here was a fellowship that had been proved
and tested. We want this kind of Christianity.
Christianity is not a matter of singing choruses
until you are absolutely exhausted, though

choruses have their place. I remember talking to
the matron of a big London hospital when I
called to see her about some aspect of Christian
work; she told me how at the Annual Meeting of
the Nurses' Christian Fellowship in that
hospital, one of the nurses had given her
testimony to the difference Christ made in her
life. But all the time the girl was speaking, the
matron was remembering what the Sisters had
to say about the work of that same nurse in the
ward, and the examination results she was
producing. Profession and performance just did
not tie up.

Are people able to depend on you?

It was a joyful love – not only mindful, and
grateful, but *joyful*. 'I thank my God upon every
remembrance of you, always in every prayer of
mine for you all making request with joy.' Are
you the kind of Christian who sends a glow
through others? I think that every time Paul
thought of the Church at Philippi a glow would
come into his face and he would smile. And
somebody would say, 'Hello, Paul, what are
you thinking about just now?' 'Oh,' he'd say,
'I'm just thinking about So-and-so at Philippi.'
With joy! Are you that kind of Christian?

Or do people say when you come in, 'Good
heavens, here she is!' Are you that dreadful kind
of person? Does the Sister on duty dance with
joy when she knows that *you* are going to be in
her ward for the next three months? Or does she
wish you far enough away? Is the Sunday
School Superintendent absolutely delighted
every time you come in *on time*? Is he so pleased

to see you? Or does he see you coming in during the singing of the first verse of the first hymn: 'There she is again – late as usual!' Joyful love! – this was a wonderful fellowship, and it happened, you know: this is no fairy story. This all happened. *A life common to the fellowship, a love constraining in the fellowship* – and the reason why? There was

(iii) *A Lord central in the fellowship*

For in this lovely warm-hearted passage, the Lord is central in two references. First in verse 8 where Paul reveals the authority to which he always appeals and under which he is always living. 'God is my witness,' he says. 'I have been talking about how I think about you, and how warm a place you have in my heart, how grateful I am for all your fellowship; and God is my witness to all I have said.' *God* is my witness.

I remember once asking a day-school class, 'What does a witness do?' And a child replied, 'He says what he knows.' 'God is my witness' – saying what he knows. That was the authority under which the fellowship was living, under which Paul lived. 'God is my witness.' Not only the Lord's authority in his own life, but the Lord's activity in the life of the church ... 'your fellowship in the gospel, the furtherance of the gospel ... being confident of this very thing that *he which hath begun a good work in you will perform it*.' Here was a church were Christ was at work ... *the Lord central in the fellowship*.

We have considered THE GREETING Paul sent,

penetrating beneath that to look at the birth of
the church. We have considered THE GRATITUDE
Paul showed, and examined the bonds of the
fellowship. Finally we must look at

3. THE GROWTH HE SEEKS (vv. 9–11)

Here we find the burden of a suppliant.
Although everything at Philippi was wonderful,
Paul was never satisfied – and neither is God.
So Paul goes on, seeking the growth of this
church, 'This I pray', and asked three things.
First of all, in verses 9–11, he prayed for

(i) *That profusion which is the measure of love*

'That your love may abound yet more and
more.' Here is the exercise of a love unselfish in
its concern for others. The picture is that of a
bucket standing under a streamlet with the water
pouring over on every side, overflowing out to
others. Love is a great giver! Here is, too, an
extravagance in love which is unrestrained ...
'that your love may abound yet more and more'.
Love never asks 'how little can I?' but 'how
much may I?' That is *the profusion which is the
measure of love*.

Paul prayed, too for

(ii) *That perception which guides the ministry of love*

'That your love may abound yet more and
more in *all knowledge and all judgment*, that you
may approve things that are excellent.' Spiritual
perception guides the ministry of love. Phillips'

translation reads, 'A love that is full of knowledge and wise insight.' There are two things involved here – first, the intimacy in which love grows. 'That your love may abound yet more and more in knowledge.' One of the fundamental blunders many Christians make is that of attempting to love a Lord they do not know. If love is to abound it must do so in the environment of knowledge.

It is here that the significance of our daily Quiet Times lies, fostering the intimacy in which love grows, and also the insight by which love knows – the wise insight of love! How much clumsy and bungling Christian work there is today, not guided by the wise insight of love. Here Paul is thinking of a love which does not need to be told because it *knows*. Are you that kind of Christian, not needing to be *told* what to do, even by the Lord, or by your minister, because you *know* by a wise insight? *That is the perception which guides the ministry of love;*

And Paul prayed, further, for

(iii) *That perfection which is the 'must' of love*

'That ye may be sincere and without offence, being filled with the fruits of righteousness which are by Jesus Christ unto the praise and glory of God.' Here is the standard that love sets – *perfection*. We are frightened of that word, but God is not. We shall never achieve it on our own human resources, but we can at least aspire to it.

Perfection! Here is a mother stitching

garments, tiny garments, for her first baby. What is her standard? I'll tell you; it's perfection. Here is a girl going out to meet her sweetheart. She spends a long time in front of the mirror before she goes down and out. What is her standard? Perfection. Mind you, some girls never achieve it, but how hard they try! Here is a bride going to her wedding: how long does she take to get ready before she goes out to the great day of her life? She takes hours! What is her standard? Perfection.

If it be true that some of us, as evangelicals, have reached the stage where we think sin just does not matter, let us look, listen, and learn. Here is the standard that love sets – perfection: not necessarily of achievement, but always of intention. And here is the secret that love has. For Paul comes back, as he always came back, to the Source and Secret of it all. He does not say vaguely and up in the air, 'That ye may be sincere and without offence being filled with the fruits of righteousness.' He goes on to say, 'which are by – *by* – Jesus Christ unto the glory and praise of God.'

So Paul comes back to where he began. He began with 'all the saints in Christ'; he ends by affirming that all they are going to be and do will be 'by Christ'. Just so, everything that you and I are as Christians begins with Christ, and all we shall ever be will be due to Christ. All the praise and glory will go to him.

What a church! What a fellowship! What a prayer! Is that your kind of church? It will be if you are that kind of Christian.

12 But I would ye should understand, brethren, that the things *which happened* unto me have fallen out rather unto the furtherance of the gospel;

13 So that my bonds in Christ are manifest in all the palace, and in all other *places;*

14 And many of the brethren in the Lord, waxing confident by my bonds, are much more bold to speak the word without fear.

15 Some indeed preach Christ even of envy and strife; and some also of good will:

16 The one preach Christ of contention, not sincerely, supposing to add affliction to my bonds:

17 But the other of love, knowing that I am set for the defence of the gospel.

18 What then? notwithstanding, every way, whether in pretence, or in truth, Christ is preached; and I therein do rejoice, yea, and will rejoice.

19 For I know that this shall turn to my salvation through your prayer, and the supply of the Spirit of Jesus Christ,

20 According to my earnest expectation and *my* hope, that in nothing I shall be ashamed, but *that* with all boldness, as always, *so* now also Christ shall be magnified in my body, whether *it be* by life, or by death.

21 For to me to live *is* Christ, and to die *is* gain.

22 But if I live in the flesh, this *is* the fruit of my labour: yet what I shall choose I wot not.

23 For I am in a strait betwixt two, having a desire to depart, and to be with Christ; which is far better:

24 Nevertheless to abide in the flesh *is* more needful for you.

25 And having this confidence, I know that I shall abide and continue with you all for your furtherance and joy of faith;

26 That your rejoicing may be more abundant in Jesus Christ for me by my coming to you again.

2

JOY – AND THE PLACE I'M IN

FOR OUR SECOND STUDY we take the section, 1: 12–26. These verses seem to belong together because of their particularly personal emphasis. Beginning at verse 12 with the phrase, 'I would ye should understand, brethren, that the things which happened unto *me* have fallen out rather unto the furtherance of the gospel', and right through this section, the words *I, me* and *my* recur with remarkable frequency. At verse 27, however, the tone changes with the very first phrase; 'Only let *your* behaviour be as it becometh the gospel of Christ.' It seems that at that point there is a change of theme in the mind of the apostle. In this chapter, therefore, we will confine ourselves to verses 12–26.

Paul was writing from Rome. That seems to be the generally accepted interpretation of the fact that he was in bonds. We know, of course, that he was in bonds and in prison elsewhere than in Rome, but the traditional view seems to be the one we can most happily accept.

Paul had had a very prolonged period of confinement. Already he had spent about two years as a prisoner back in the home country; there had been the long voyage to Italy: there remained still two further years of captivity in a house in Rome itself. Every moment of day and night had been shared, at any rate in Rome, by at least one soldier of the Imperial Guard, to whom Paul was chained.

It was no easy place to be in, no easy situation. Yet right in the middle of it this man says, 'I therein do rejoice, yea, and will rejoice.' Here is a man *singing in a difficult place*. Does this possibly identify one of our problems? We meet so often the attitude – 'It's all very well for you, but you don't work where I work.' 'You're not in the ward where I am on duty.' 'You're not in the school where I teach.' 'You don't live in the town where I live.' 'You haven't the boss I've got.' 'It's all very well for you to talk about living a life continually sustained by joy, but you wouldn't rejoice if you were where I am.' That is a common attitude to life; we feel that just because we are in a certain difficult place, that justifies out failure to rejoice!

I am not going to suggest that I can teach you much about this, but let us see how Paul got on. I know your place may be quite difficult, but I do not think you have had your boss chained to you for two years! However difficult your boss may be, I am quite certain he is no more difficult than a soldier of the Imperial Guard. 'The things that have happened unto me' – the song of the difficult place.

Paul is writing very freely, very intimately; and rather unusually he is beginning with his own situation. But then the Philippians were concerned about him. They had sent a messenger to find out how he was getting on, and so in effect he was only replying to their concern and their interest. That is why, I think, in this particular letter he begins by writing such a lot about himself.

Three things blend into the whole experience of Paul as he writes, and these are three things worth considering in any difficult place. I believe we can sense in the writing here that there could be

1. A BITTERNESS THAT CAN SPOIL

When you are in a difficult place it is very easy to become bitter, and I have never yet met a bitter person who rejoices. The two things do not blend. If one is bitter, one is usually a miserable kind of person. Is there a root of bitterness in some part of *your* life, which is spoiling the whole?

What, for Paul, entered into this potential bitterness? He had wonderfully overcome it; he had risen above it, and was rejoicing. But potentially the bitterness was there. What was involved that could have made Paul an extremely bitter man? I think there were three strands in that potential bitterness:

(i) *The sheer unfairness of his bonds*

In verse 13 Paul speaks of 'my bonds in
Christ' and it is very easy to gloss over that
phrase – 'my bonds', this chain on my wrist; this
guard in my room day and night. My bonds!
The sheer injustice of them!

Thrice already Paul had heard the verdict of
authority. When he was arrested, the Captain of
the Temple Guard said, 'This man has nothing
laid to his charge worthy of death or of bonds.'
When he came up for trial before Festus, the
new Governor in Syria and Palestine, Festus
said, 'This man has committed nothing worthy
of death.' Finally, when Paul appeared before
Agrippa and Festus and they consulted together,
they said, 'This man doeth nothing worthy of
death or of bonds.' Yet here he is in Rome, a
prisoner, and in bonds. This was something in
Paul's life stamped with unfairness and injustice.
And he had known it for so long!

It is not easy to sing when you have been
treated unjustly and unfairly. You were due for
promotion but it wasn't given you and you are
still in the same job. You should have been
getting better pay now, but you are not. You
should have been in a different office, but you
are in the same one. Grossly unfair; quite
unjust! You were promised a job; you never got
it. When you married, you anticipated living in
a certain house. You put everything you could
into that house, and then your husband was
moved, so you had to move too. Most unfair
after all the trouble you had gone to, the hopes
you had cherished. You made your plans for

your children's education, but the whole thing
has to be scrapped. The bitterness of resentment
can easily creep into a situation stamped with
unfairness and injustice.

Are you like that? Is there bitterness in your
heart, your mind, your soul, are you resentful?
You are not rejoicing. The poison is right
through your home, right through your job, into
your church; it is everywhere. You are a bitter
man, a bitter woman, because of the injustice of
the place where you are. The sheer unfairness of
undeserved bonds.

There was a second strand in the potential
bitterness in Paul's heart and life:

(ii) *The subtle unfriendliness of his colleagues*

I do not think I am reading into this passage
anything that is not there. Look at verse 15.
'Some preach Christ even of envy and strife.'
These were Christians, and they were preaching
Christ. They were not preaching heresy. Some
Christian people in Rome were apparently
making the most of the situation in which Paul
was placed, serving their own ends. With Paul
out of the way they were making the most of
their opportunity, getting themselves into
positions of strong influence. Sound enough!
entirely orthodox! preaching Christ! but
elbowing Paul out and rubbing this fact in,
'supposing to add irritation and annoyance to my
bonds'. The danger here is not resentment, but
jealousy.

Have you ever known this experience? Maybe
you had been on furlough, and when you got

back to the mission field you found that during
your absence somebody you did not particularly
like, and who obviously did not like you, had
wormed his way into the very centre of the
work. He was doing the kind of job you had
done, *and* was being recognized and accepted.
You had been elbowed out! How did you accept
that? Did bitterness creep into your heart and
into your relationships?

It may be that illness kept you out of church
work for a while. You could not go along to the
women's meeting and Mrs So-and-so took her
chance. Now she is on the committee, and
running the affair! You used to be the one to
whom everyone turned for advice, but now they
turn to her. And she does not mind letting you
know it! Oh, she does not say anything but some
of her friends do, and the fact is rubbed in. The
subtle unfriendliness of colleagues!

There is such a thing as jealousy in Christian
work. A new minister comes into the town.
Possibly you had been getting a little bit slack in
your own ministry, not preparing as thoroughly
as you used to; not praying as much; and some
of those rather loosely-attached Christians that
are found in every community hived off from
you and went along to the new man. They come
back and tell you, 'My word, we had such a
blessing last Sunday from Mr So-and-so.' They
never said that to you! The subtle unfriendliness
of colleagues!

So it was with Paul: jealousy could so easily
have arisen. Paul could have looked at those
men, preaching Christ where he would have

been doing it if he had been free; he could have hated them for robbing him of a place that was his by right. Is there somebody that you do not like because deep down you are jealous? That person has wormed his way into a situation which you feel is yours by right. There is no good to be found in talking about rejoicing, is there? – not so long as So-and-so is preaching Christ out of envy and strife, adding affliction to your bonds. You cannot rejoice there, can you?

The third strand in Paul's potential bitterness was more disturbing still:

(iii) *The seeming unfaithfulness of his Lord*

Resentment, jealousy, and now doubt. This is not specifically stated here, but surely it must have been in the mind of Paul, one of the weapons that the enemy of souls would use to cripple this great warrior. 'What about unanswered prayer, Paul? Two years in jail, back there in Palestine; the long sea voyage as a prisoner; and now two years in bonds again. This is something that has gone on a long time. You have been in prison before, but not for as long as this. You have prayed about it; others have prayed; but God has not done a thing!'

But not only was prayer unanswered: there was a mighty potential lying here unused. Who was this man, so long confined? He was a great preacher, and he was silenced; a man with preaching in his very blood and his very bones, a man called by God to preach and he could not open his mouth! Here was a pioneer, a great strategist of the church, and he was confined to one room with four walls, and he could not get out! The only marching Paul ever knew now was the tramp of feet passing by outside! He was anchored, fettered, bound to one room: he could not move. The man who had journeyed endlessly for Christ, and had founded churches here, there, and everywhere, could go nowhere. The seeming unfaithfulness of his Lord – where was God's purpose in all this? Paul had been called to be an apostle, not to be a prisoner. He had been called to preach, and he could preach no longer.

This writer, then, is no theorist. This man who says, 'I therein do rejoice, yea, and will rejoice' is a man talking out of a place a thousand times more difficult than your place. I do not care what your place is; it is not more difficult than Paul's.

Such is the threefold *bitterness that can spoil*, in the difficult place. But secondly, we can find here

2. A BLESSEDNESS THAT CAN SURPRISE

The situation was hurtful: but Paul found that as well as being hurtful it was helpful too. So we find that he goes on to complete verse 12: 'The things which have happened unto me have fallen out rather unto the furtherance of the gospel.' That was the thing that surprised him – or maybe it did not. Perhaps Paul was so sensitive to the mind of Christ that nothing would surprise him. After all, the man who said, 'All things work together for good to them that

love God' must have included even this, when
he had to practise what he preached. Sometimes
some of us preachers find it very difficult to
practise what we preach, but Paul was practising
it now. 'The things which have happened unto
me have fallen out rather unto *the furtherance of
the gospel*.' What was the blessedness of this
difficult place that startled and surprised both
Paul and the church?

First of all there was

(i) *An Opportunity given for the Gospel*

'My bonds in Christ are manifest in all the
Imperial Guard' (v. 13). The general consensus
of opinion seems to be that the word here
translated 'palace' is a Greek word that
primarily is related not to buildings but to
people. It seems that Paul has discovered that
from his prison chamber he is reaching people
who might otherwise never have been reached.
He was getting the gospel into the picked
Imperial Guard; the *élite* regiment of Rome was
being evangelized from a room. The chain
which deprived him of his liberty gave him his
opportunity – an opportunity granted for the
gospel.

One at a time, or possibly two at a time, the
Imperial Guard was chained by the wrist to Paul
the Apostle. In the hours of solitude, no doubt
they conversed; while in company with others
the guard *must* listen while Paul discussed and
preached. What an opportunity!

I wonder if this is something that some of us
have to learn. You never wanted to live in that

town. Ever since you went there you have
resented it, resented leaving your church,
resented leaving your friends, resented the fact
that your husband had moved, had got a new
job, that your children had to change their
school. You still don't want to live in that town.
But I tell you this: God wants you to live
there. Can you dare turn round and say to God,
'I don't want to live here; I hate it'? I want to
ask you this. Is it possible there is someone
living in the same street, a neighbour, who
would never hear the gospel of Jesus Christ if it
wasn't that God called a Christian person to live
next door? They have never had a Christian
living next door before, but *you* are living there
now. Is that why God moved your husband?

You never wanted to go into hospital. You
certainly did not want that operation, that long
convalescence. You hated hospital. But there
was a nurse there who had never been to church
since she left Sunday School. Or was there a
patient going into the same ward whom God
wanted to reach? How could he do it unless he
sent a Christian? So you went! I want to suggest
that whenever God puts you and me in a
difficult place it is because there are people to be
touched there for him.

An opportunity granted for the gospel! That is
something of a surprise, something to make us
begin to sing. We have been wrapped up in
ourselves, our resentment, our jealousy, our
doubt: here is a golden opportunity right at our
feet, immediately at our door. You did not want
to teach in that school; you have been a bitter,

resentful Christian ever since you went there. But you are the only teacher on the staff who is a Christian, the only one going to teach Christ to some of those little folk!

Then secondly there was the blessed surprise of

(ii) *A Ministry achieved in the Church*

In verse 14 Paul says that 'many of the brethren, waxing confident by my bonds, are much more bold to speak the Word without fear'. Not only was there an opportunity granted for the gospel then, but a ministry was being achieved in the church.

'Many of the brethren ...' I wonder whether you have stopped to think that there is a ministry that you and I are to exercise towards other Christians. Many good keen Christians are quite aware that they have a ministry to the unsaved, quite prepared to recognize their responsibility towards those who never come to church. But they have no awareness at all that they have a ministry to other Christians.

I remember being taught a lesson about this when I started in Christian work many years ago. I had graduated from Edinburgh University and for two years I worked on the staff of the Children's Special Service Mission. Among my duties was arranging meetings for the then President of the C.S.S.M. and Scripture Union, Bishop Taylor Smith, in Aberdeen. I was a very junior worker; he was a very revered and wonderful Christian man. It was the first time we had met. I told him the arrangements I had

made, where he was going to speak, what kind
of a reception he would be likely to have. But he
turned and said, 'I want to ask you something.'

Bishop Taylor Smith had a most awkward
habit of waiting for an answer when he asked a
question. Some people do not: they ask, and go
on talking: he always waited. His question was:
'Have you sanctified yourself for me?' Well,
what would *you* have said! I did not know what
to say, nor even what he meant! He went on to
say, 'Look here, we are going to be working
together. Our Lord sanctified himself for the
disciples who worked with him – he set himself
apart to be a blessing to them. And I expect that
you are going to be a blessing to me, and *I*
expect to be a blessing to you. Have you
sanctified yourself for me?' I said, 'Well, sir, I
am sorry but I never thought of it like that.'
Then he said, 'Here is a prayer that will help
you to remember – a prayer of five words: *For
thee, For them. Amen.*'

A ministry in the church! Do you realize that
you have a ministry to other Christians? Not a
ministry of the gospel, but truly a ministry of
the grace of God – the adequacy of it, the
sufficiency of it, the glory of it, the wonder of
it, the victory of it – a ministry to other
Christians. You are not in your present situation
just for the unconverted you may reach, but also
for the Christians you may help. But how are
you to exercise that ministry unless first of all
you yourself have been tried and tested?

Even Paul did not realize all that was at stake
in his imprisonment. Paul was thinking of the

brethren in Rome: but God was thinking of something infinitely greater. This ministry achieved in the church, by which many of the brethren were waxing confident, and were being blessed and becoming active, this ministry has not ended yet! For if Paul had not been in prison, the prison epistles would never have been written and a great part of our New Testament would never have come into existence. Paul was put into prison not in order that he might preach, but that he might write. Here is a ministry by Paul that has gone right on and on and that will never end until we are in glory. That ministry achieved in the church was part of the blessedness that startles and surprises us as we look into his difficult place.

Does God want you to exercise a ministry to others? Remember how in the New Testament we read of being able to comfort others with the comfort with which we ourselves were comforted. God puts you into a situation, not just that you can reach folk with the gospel, but in order that, out of that situation, you may minister to other Christians. It may be that there *is* another Christian on the staff of that school, and you do not know it. His light is hid under a bushel and nobody on the staff ever dreamed he was converted until you arrived. Then things started happening to you, that were difficult for *you* but stung *him* into life, and he has emerged as a Christian. You found to your joy that he was converted too. A ministry achieved in the church!

The third blessedness that can surprise in such a situation as Paul's is

(iii) *A Quality secured in the Life*

Look at verse 19. 'For I know that this shall turn to my salvation through your prayer, and the supply of the Spirit of Jesus Christ.' There are various interpretations of the word 'salvation' in this particular verse. The one that seems to me most natural is this: Paul realized that in this difficult place not only was an opportunity being granted to reach the unsaved; not only was a ministry being achieved to strengthen the church; but a quality and a purpose of grace was being fulfilled in his own soul. He was in prison not only for the sake of the Imperial Guard, not only for the sake of the church at Rome: Paul was in prison for Paul's sake, also.

'This shall turn to my salvation' – to my full spiritual health – 'through your prayer and the supply of the Spirit.' A quality of life was going to be secured in Paul that could not be secured in any other way: a completeness, a maturity, a Christlikeness.

Will you pardon here a personal reference that may illustrate the point? I had the misfortune – and I think I can call it a misfortune – to preach to crowded congregations in all the earlier years of my ministry. In my father's church, and when I was a staff worker on the C.S.S.M., God graciously gave me some wonderful times. Then as a curate in Broadwater, and later as Vicar in St. James', Carlisle, I always had a full church.

That privilege has its perils: any man who preaches to a crowd all his life is in a dangerous position. It is not so much *what* a man preaches to a crowd, but *how* he preaches. In one of my early churches I remember hearing the kind of backwash remark that comes to a minister by a devious route, that one particular member of the congregation had said 'I do object to being shouted at!'

I think I was sincere in my ministry in those early days; I think I was faithful in the truth I proclaimed; but I know there was something lacking in the tone of my voice if not in the truth of the message. Then God took me out of crowded churches and put me down in a little empty church in Edinburgh, where, before I went, a good morning congregation was 30, and a good evening congregation 20; the Sunday School amounted to 18 children, and there was nothing going on in the church from Sunday night till Sunday morning. All my friends said, 'You are making the biggest mistake of your life in going to Edinburgh.' During the first eighteen months of my ministry there I was offered very nearly eight other churches. That very rarely happens when a minister settles in a new church: usually he is left in peace, at any rate for some time. But I was offered these other churches, some of them with stipends double what I was getting.

Now I had thought God took me to that empty church to build it up, and I believe he did. But I came to realize that he took me to that empty church to do something for George

Duncan, the Rector. You see, you can flog a full church, and you will flog it empty; but you cannot flog an empty church full! You will never fill it that way. There had been a grace lacking before, and God wanted me to find it.

'This shall turn to ... salvation.' There may be qualities lacking in your life as a Christian that God can only secure if he puts you in a place utterly difficult, desperately lonely, where doubt beats in upon your soul, where jealousy is tending to thrust up its angry, ugly head, where resentment's fires are liable to burst into flame. That is the very place that is going to turn to your salvation. God is going to do something to you that will make you sweet and gracious and lovely. He cannot do it anywhere except in the fire, so he puts you there, where the difficult situation can turn to your greater salvation.

An opportunity for the gospel, a ministry to the church, and a quality secured in one's life are enough to transform the most trying circumstances with a blessedness that can surprise.

Then, thirdly, we must notice in this section about the place Paul was in –

3. A BOLDNESS THAT CAN SING

Even in this passage, the theme recurring again and again is that of rejoicing – I joy and rejoice – a boldness that can sing. Some of us sing so long as the sun shines: the moment the clouds arrive we begin not to sing but to grouse. Paul is a brave man, a courageous man. I think

we should remember sometimes that courage has
its place in Christian experience.

Who was it told, of a visit to a mission field,
that when he came to a particular station, at the
very first meal he saw a young lady missionary sit-
ting there, looking very quiet, very alone, and
wondered why? Then he gathered that the
young husband, with whom she had not been
out on the field very long, had just died. But
that very day, the young widow had received a
cable from her godly mother at home: in it were
two words – 'Be brave'. Not love, not sympathy
just the words 'be brave'! The boldness that can
sing!

We need this in the church. So many of us,
the moment we are up against things, curl up
and give up. It is all right being a Christian in a
crowd where everybody is singing, but to be
alone .... Be brave! 'My earnest expectation and
my hope, that in nothing I shall be ashamed,
but that with all boldness, as always, so now also
Christ shall be magnified' (v. 20).

Three things went into this boldness. First,

(i) *Paul's concern for God's glory*

'That now also Christ shall be magnified in
my body' – that Christ shall be 'made great'.
Utterly forgetful of himself, Paul's one concern
was for another, and that Other his Lord; that
Christ be made visible, apparent, obvious. His
anxiety was, not that Paul should be heard, but
that Christ should be seen; not that Paul should
be free, but that Christ should be found; not
that Paul should be responsible for a great work,

but that men should be reached in a mighty blessing. His whole concern was that Christ should be magnified.

Paul's boldness was apparent, too, in his

(ii) *Contempt for his own comfort*

The place he was in was not only difficult, it was dangerous. A very real threat of uncertainty hung over the whole situation. Life was possible, but equally so was death; Paul was ready for either. He said, 'I couldn't care less; in fact, I'd rather go, I'd rather die.'

There is concern here for Christ's glory: there is contempt for Paul's own comfort, and there is, besides, a great

(iii) *Confidence in God's control*

'I am in a strait betwixt two', he said, (v. 23) meaning, 'I am in a situation where I am quite helpless; I am hemmed in; I'd love to go; I'd love to die. I know the other alternative is to live. *But* if I am helpless in this situation, it is still under control. Having this confidence (v. 25) I know that I shall abide and continue with you all for your furtherance and joy of faith, for this is more needful for you.'

Paul had assessed it all: he had realized that Christ was in control, and although it was not an easy place, he felt sure that the thing that was more needful, not the thing that was most comfortable, was the thing that would happen. *A concern for God's glory; a contempt for Paul's comfort; and a confidence in God's control* – what boldness they engender – boldness that can sing!

A difficult place? Yes, maybe. It wasn't the first time, though, that Paul had sung praises in prison. Oh, Christian, in the difficult place, learn to sing with Paul!

Such is Paul's recipe for rejoicing in 'whatever place I'm in': an antidote to *the bitterness that can spoil*; the expectation of *a blessedness that can surprise*; the secret of *a boldness that can sing.* 'Therein I rejoice ... yea, and will rejoice.'

27 Only let your conversation be as it becometh the gospel of Christ: that whether I come and see you, or else be absent, I may hear of your affairs, that ye stand fast in one spirit, with one mind striving together for the faith of the gospel;

28 And in nothing terrified by your adversaries: which is to them an evident token of perdition, but to you of salvation, and that of God.

29 For unto you it is given in the behalf of Christ, not only to believe on him, but also to suffer for his sake;

30 Having the same conflict which ye saw in me, and now hear *to be* in me.

CHAPTER 2.

IF *there be* therefore any consolation in Christ, if any comfort of love, if any fellowship of the Spirit, if any bowels and mercies,

2 Fulfil ye my joy, that ye be likeminded, having the same love, *being* of one accord, of one mind.

3 *Let* nothing *be done* through strife or vainglory; but in lowliness of mind let each esteem other better than themselves.

4 Look not every man on his own things, but every man also on the things of others.

5 Let this mind be in you, which was also in Christ Jesus:

6 Who, being in the form of God, thought it not robbery to be equal with God:

7 But made himself of no reputation, and took upon him the form of a servant, and was made in the likeness of men:

8 And being found in fashion as a man, he humbled himself, and became obedient unto death, even the death of the cross.

9 Wherefore God also hath highly exalted him, and given him a name which is above every name:

10 That at the name of Jesus every knee should bow, of *things* in heaven, and *things* in earth, and *things* under the earth;

11 And *that* every tongue should confess that Jesus Christ *is* Lord, to the glory of God the Father.

12 Wherefore, my beloved, as ye have always obeyed, not as in my presence only, but now much more in my absence, work out your own salvation with fear and trembling.

13 For it is God which worketh in you both to will and to do of *his* good pleasure.

14 Do all things without murmurings and disputings:

15 That ye may be blameless and harmless, the sons of God, without rebuke, in the midst of a crooked and perverse nation, among whom ye shine as lights in the world;

16 Holding forth the word of life; that I may rejoice in the day of Christ, that I have not run in vain, neither laboured in vain.

17 Yea, and if I be offered upon the sacrifice and service of your faith, I joy, and rejoice with you all.

18 For the same cause also do ye joy, and rejoice with me.

19 But I trust in the Lord Jesus to send Timotheus shortly unto you, that I also may be of good comfort, when I know your state.

20 For I have no man likeminded, who will naturally care for your state.

21 For all seek their own, not the things which are Jesus Christ's.

22 But ye know the proof of him, that, as a son with the father, he hath served with me in the gospel.

23 Him therefore I hope to send presently, so soon as I shall see how it will go with me.

24 But I trust in the Lord that I also myself shall come shortly.

25 Yet I supposed it necessary to send to you Epaphroditus, my brother, and companion in labour, and fellowsoldier, but your messenger, and he that ministered to my wants.

26 For he longed after you all, and was full of heaviness, because that ye had heard that he had been sick.

27 For indeed he was sick nigh unto death: but God had mercy on him; and not on him only, but on me also, lest I should have sorrow upon sorrow.

28 I sent him therefore the more carefully, that, when ye see him again, ye may rejoice, and that I may be the less sorrowful.

29 Receive him therefore in the Lord with all gladness; and hold such in reputation:

30 Because for the work of Christ he was nigh unto death, not regarding his life, to supply your lack of service toward me.

3

JOY – AND THE PEOPLE
I'M WITH

WE COME to our third study and note at
once how at verse 27 of chapter 1 Paul's
theme changes: 'only let your behaviour'
('conversation' has changed its meaning, it really
means your behaviour, your conduct, including
the whole of life, both speech and attitude and
action and thought), 'only let *your* behaviour be
as it becometh the gospel of Christ'.

Paul is now approaching the question of
human relationships. This theme asserts itself
right through the following verses, and I want to
extend this section to include the incidental, and
personal, and primarily historical, references in
the second half of the second chapter. Here Paul
refers to the forthcoming visit of Timothy to
Philippi, and also to the more immediate return
of Epaphroditus: I want to take the whole
section as one.

You will see how the theme of human
relationships crops up again and again. There is
continuity right through this section. 'That ye
stand fast in one spirit, with one mind striving
together for the faith of the gospel; and in
nothing terrified by your adversaries' (1:27, 28).
'Being of one accord, of one mind. Let nothing
be done through strife or vainglory; but in
lowliness of mind let each esteem other better
than themselves. Look not every man on his
own things, but every man also on the things of
others' (2:2–4). 'Do all things without
murmurings and disputings: that ye may be
blameless and harmless, the sons of God,
without rebuke, in the midst of a crooked and
perverse nation' (2:14, 15).

The continuity holds through the section that
I am including in this study, although it could
be argued that it is not strictly part of it. But
Paul is referring to Timothy and his character,
and says, 'I have no man likeminded, who will
naturally care for your state' (2:20). And he
speaks of Epaphroditus in verse 30, 'Because for
the work of Christ he was nigh unto death, not
regarding his life, to supply your lack of service
toward me.'

I was glad to see that Bishop Handley Moule
likewise includes the final verses of chapter 2 in
this section; he, too, suggests that the same
theme is under discussion to the end of this
passage. Running right through is this thought
of human relationships; both to the world
outside, and to other Christians inside.

I am going to suggest that Christian joy and

rejoicing, the main theme of the whole letter as we saw, is very closely tied up with human relationships. Sometimes, our problem in not being able to rejoice is due to the place that we are in; but at other times it is due to *the people we are with*. So at the back of our mind, although it is not primarily emphasised here, we are thinking how it is possible to live 'the life of continual rejoicing' – with certain people, as well as in certain places.

It came to me with a sense of shock when I was engaged on a world tour of ministry to discover that on the mission field, problem number one is this very problem of relationships. The biggest difficulty on the mission field is not the relationship of the missionary to those whom he is seeking to serve. It is not the indifference of the local people, the nationals to whom he is bringing the gospel. It is not the difficulty of learning the language, not the hardship of a different climate or diet. Problem number one on the mission field is the problem of the relationship of missionary to missionary.

But this is not only a problem on the mission field. It is a problem with every Christian. I wonder how many Christians there are who have problems of relationship with other Christians in their own church, in their own fellowship, in their own assembly. Or they have problems of relationship with other Christians where they work. Or their problem is that of a right relationship with those who are not Christians.

The one thing that very often takes away the

song, out of our hearts and from our lips, is the
fact that we are not living in a right relationship
with other people. There is a maladjustment,
like a dislocation of a bone, and so long as the
dislocation remains there is no ease, there is no
comfort.

Paul is getting down now, not so much to a
problem that exists urgently in the church to
which he is writing, but to one which, as he is
so very urgently aware, is bound to crop up
sooner or later, and to become of vital
importance, even if it has not already done
so.

This question of right relationships between
Christians, and between the Christian and the
world, is important for two reasons.

First of all the relationship of Christian to
Christian is important *on the grounds of witness*.
This problem of human relationships is the
major problem the world faces – the problem of
relationships between employer and employee;
between nation and nation; between class and
class; between husband and wife; between
parents and children. This problem of human
relationships, outside in the world, is one that
baffles and defies solution. The world wants to
know, Is there an answer to this? Our Lord,
indeed, has tied up the question of Christian
unity with Christian witness. He prays, you
remember, 'that they may be one, *that the world
may believe*'.

If the world has no solution to this problem,
where can it find it? Can it find it in the church?
Well, if the world turns to the church, it finds

that the church is up against exactly the same problem too, and apparently has no solution. Why bother about the church then, if the church has not the answer?

Has Communism the answer? Is there a unity within the Communist world that does not exist outside? Is that why men were at one time turning to Communism? They did not know the price at which that apparent unity had been achieved, nor how soon the Communist world itself would be divided, yet for a time Communist solidarity was impressive. It seemed to solve problems. Is the church's witness to unity any more impressive?

This problem of relationship is important also *because of the question of joy*. Whatever else can be said about disunity between Christians, I question if we can ever praise the Lord for it. Have you ever been able to kneel down and say 'O Lord, Hallelujah, I'm not on speaking terms with So-and-So'? Have you ever been able to rejoice because you are not on speaking terms? You just cannot praise for disunity and dislocation in relationships. The joy goes, the song dies.

Bishop Handley Moule has this very pertinent comment to make on any break of unity between Christians: 'This never happens where there has not been grievous sin in the matter, on the one side, or on the other, or both.'

Precisely: and the reason you and I cannot sing and praise when there is disunity, a break of relationships, a loss of fellowship between us and another Christian, is because there is sin

around – either in us, or in them, or most likely
in both.

This question of relationships is a very
practical one and a vital one. Sometimes we
think it does not matter; but Paul is acutely
aware of it; and in this lovely church at Philippi,
so full of promise, Paul is anxious and
concerned that this question of relationships
should never spoil the work, should never halt
it, should never disrupt it.

And so he gets down to it in this section. Let
us look at it, and break the passage into its
various significant and relevant parts. First of
all, in this passage there are

1. THE STRESSES DISCERNED

There are certain stresses in relationships that
Paul is concerned about. The first is this: there
is going to be, there must be, there has already
been and in some measure, there most certainly
will continue to be

(i) *Opposition from without*

Paul speaks of 'your adversaries' (1:28). There
will be a ceaseless pressure from the enemy of
souls against the church. There is going to be a
continuous attack from the enemy from without
upon the fellowship of the Christian church.
Paul's word concerning this is 'stand fast'. Let
there be no retreat. Present a united front.

Nothing brings more confusion, more
disorder, more disunity into Christian fellowship
than a wholesale retreat on a section of the front.

It means, inevitably, a break in fellowship. One of the simple, elementary tactics of warfare is – divide, and then destroy. Break the unity, and then make the most of the disunity. Paul says to this church, 'When you are facing pressure from without, from the world or from the Devil, do not retreat; stand fast; do not give way.'

May I indicate the kind of situation that could happen? When they bring maybe a sweepstake ticket around in the office, or in the factory, or some course of action is suggested which challenges Christian standards: some Christians give way, others stand firm. What happens? You get a break of fellowship right away.

We are living in days when the Christian church, by and large, is on the retreat. We are giving ground right, left, and centre. Disunity is creeping into our Christian fellowships. Why is it that people retreat? Always it is because they do not want to suffer, to be laughed at; they are anxious not to be thought peculiar, not to be criticized, not to be ridiculed. So they give way and they give in. Paul suggests, 'Remember this. It's part of your privilege: when you are facing opposition, and the ceaseless pressure from the world and the Devil, it is part of your privilege as a Christian to suffer.'

Never think that the only thing about being a Christian is believing; it is suffering too. Paul says 'unto you it is given in the behalf of Christ, not only to believe on him, but also to suffer for his sake' (1:29).

If there are young folk reading this who want to be popular, want to be hail-fellow-well-met in

C

the crowd where they work, then for pity's sake
let them stop thinking about being a real
Christian! Our Lord said, 'The servant is not
greater than his lord. If they have persecuted me
they will persecute you.' Once you are sure that
you have reached ground upon which you must
take a stand – and some Christians stand upon
ground that they need never stand on – but if
you are certain that you have ground that you
must stand on, then *stand*, and stand together.

If *opposition from without* is the first stress affect-
ing Christian relationships that Paul is concerned
about, the second is

(ii) *Corruption from within*

'Let nothing be done through selfish ambition
or the seeking for personal prestige' (2:3). If
retreat breaks fellowship, self-advancement
breaks it too. This again was not necessarily
actually happening in Philippi; his words
express an anxiety that Paul felt, born out of his
wide experience of the Christian church.

How often disunity arises, and therefore
danger to the fellowship, not because of a retreat
in face of the enemy, but because of some
personal advancement sought by a Christian
here or a Christian there – by the kind of person
whose opinion must always be deferred to
because he is always right; the kind of Christian
who has a perfect right to criticize others but
you must not criticize her – that is an insult; the
kind of Christian who must run everything, and
be in control; the kind of Christian who is
always   talking,   always   pushing   forward,

dominating committees, dominating groups, dominating meetings, self-asserting.

If it is dangerous in warfare to have a great wedge driven in the front line where some have retreated, it is equally dangerous to push out a narrow salient where a tiny segment has penetrated forward. Both are threats to the solidity and the unity of the whole front, and likewise stresses that can break Christian fellowship. They can arise from opposition from without, if we are going to retreat; they can come from corruption from within, if we are going to allow the old nature, the self, to push itself forward until *we* are prominent, until *we* are always doing things in the church and no one else is doing anything!

So, the stresses being discerned, is there any answer? We move on to

2. THE SECRETS DESCRIBED

These are two. First of all Paul is assuming here, and asserting, and re-stating, and underlining

(i) *The presence of a life*

We are to stand fast *in* the one Holy Spirit (1:27). We are to exercise the same love (2:2). That is to say, we are here stressing something we stressed before in our first study, that we have not only a new life, the same life in us all, but we also have a new love, and it is selfless.

The life we have is strong, as strong as the Spirit himself; the love we have is selfless, as

selfless as the Christ. This is not something that
the world can produce, because the world has
neither the life nor the love. That is why it is a
lot of nonsense to talk about all men being
brothers – they are not all brothers. But all
Christians are; they are brothers and sisters in
Christ, through *the presence of a common life*.
That is Paul's first secret.

Secondly, we find, I think, the most
challenging secret of all:

(ii) *The absence of a limit*

Having spoken of the one Spirit, having
spoken of the same love, having spoken of the
need of maintaining the one mind, Paul says, 'In
order to do this, let us look at the mind that is
in you' – the mind of Christ.

In verses 5–11 of chapter 2 we come to a
passage to which theologians have given much
attention; one of the great passages concerning
the nature and person of our Lord. But I want
to note that Paul's concern here was not
primarily with theology at all, but with Christian
conduct. He was not trying to set out a
wonderful picture of the person of Christ; he
was not concerned with the portrait of a person
– he was concerned with the example of the
indwelling mind that was theirs.

What is the mind of Christ? What is the way
of Christ that you and I can follow if we are
going to discover the secret of maintaining
unity? He was One truly God yet truly Man. He
followed the path of utter selflessness, holding
on to nothing grimly as his right, but instead

accepting the uttermost depths of degradation, in the purpose of God and in his love for the world. Being in the form of God he became obedient in an ever descending scale of humiliation, in the will of God and in his love for humanity, until he became obedient unto death and that not an ordinary death, but the death of the Cross.

The thought which comes to me, with tremendous challenge, is this: what Paul is getting at here is that the mind which was in Christ was a mind which set no limit to the amount of injury it was prepared to receive. Christ never said to the Father, 'I will go so far and no further.' He could not have gone further than he went; he could not have suffered more than he did; he could not have been more insulted and degraded than he was. He who was in the form of God, the One who had the right to all the adoration, the worship, the praise, the obedience of the whole human race, took upon himself the sum total of their disobedience and their hatred – he took it *all*.

Let that mind be in you. When your injuries and insults and wrongs exceed the injuries and insults and wrongs of your Master, then maybe you will have the right to call a halt, but not until then!

What causes a break in fellowship between Christians? One thing only. An unforgiving spirit; the setting of a limit as to how much injury I am prepared to take from somebody; how much criticism I am prepared to bear; how much comment, gossip, talk I will allow to go on. The moment I set a limit, the moment I nurture an unforgiving spirit, at that very moment the song dies.

Do you remember what our Lord said in the parable about the two servants? One was forgiven a vast sum of money that he could never hope to repay: and that man, having been forgiven such a vast sum, went straight away to another servant who owed him a paltry amount, and refused to forgive him.

I preached a sermon on that and I entitled it, 'Forgiven but Unforgiving'. Is that true of any Christian here? Forgiven so much; but unforgiving. Is there someone with whom you are not on speaking terms? You have not forgiven them something they did, something they said? Do you remember what our Lord said about this? 'If ye forgive not men their trespasses, neither will your Father forgive your trespasses' (Matt. 6: 15). He is not talking about salvation there; he is talking about fellowship. If you will not forgive somebody who has wronged you, not only do you lose fellowship with him but you lose fellowship with God.

No wonder the song dies. Out of fellowship with another believer: out of fellowship with my divine Lord – how can I sing? How can I rejoice? How can I praise? 'I'll forgive her but I don't want to have any more to do with her.' Have you ever spoken like that? And you thought you were generous: you thought you were wonderful: you thought you were being Christian: you thought you were quite outstanding, quite unique! 'I'll forgive her, but I

don't want to have any more to do with her.'
Listen for a moment to these words: 'Forgive us
our debts as we forgive our debtors.' 'As we
forgive.' '*As we forgive*.' 'O God, I am so sorry I
did that; please forgive me.' And a voice from
heaven says, 'I'll forgive you, but *I don't want to
have any more to do with you!*'

That is not forgiveness at all.

A mind which sets no limit to the amount of
injury it is prepared to receive: are you like that?
You will be a happy Christian if you are. You
will have nothing to grouse about; you will have
no complaints about other people.

'Let this mind be in you' presupposes the
presence of a life. It is only because we are
indwelt by the one Spirit; only because we have
the same love, the divine love; only because of
the presence of the life, that there can be the
absence of a limit. It's a very simple secret, is
it not? The stresses once discerned, the secret is
soon described; there follows

3. THE SEQUEL DESIRED

Why is Paul concerned about this? For two
reasons. Leaving the great Christological passage
where, having described the humiliation of
Christ, Paul has gone on to describe the
transcendent glory that God will give to him
because of his humiliation, in verse 12 he says
'Wherefore, my beloved, as ye have always
obeyed, not as in my presence only, but now
much more in my absence, work out your own

salvation with fear and trembling. For it is God
which worketh in you both to will and to do of
his good pleasure. Do all things without
murmurings and disputings: that ye may be
blameless and harmless, the sons of God,
without rebuke, in the midst of a crooked and
perverse nation, among whom ye shine as lights
in the world; holding forth the word of life; that
I may rejoice in the day of Christ, that I have
not run in vain, neither laboured in vain.' Such
is *the sequel desired*.

The first sequel that Paul was so jealous
about, and which was involved in this question
of right relationships was

(i) *A continuing progress*

'Work out your own salvation with fear and
trembling' (v. 12). The thought here is not so
much 'work out from within', but work out to
its completion, work out to the end. Work out
your own salvation; don't be halted in your
Christian development and growth. Work it out
until the whole job is done.

I do not know anything which brings
Christians so quickly to a dead halt as broken,
wrong relationships, either with other Christians,
or with the world. I am sure that every minister
knows what it is to have a most promising
member of the church growing rapidly, until
suddenly something goes wrong and he comes
to a dead stop. All the promise seems to die in a
night, and he is right out of things. Perhaps
there was a row with the minister, or a
disagreement with a deacon, or somebody was

heard to say something, or somebody asked him to move out of his pew in the church.

Fancy leaving a church because somebody asked you to move out of a pew! I know it was a *most* discourteous thing for the person to do; it was a *horrible* experience to have anybody ask you to move out of your seat in a church. But it was an even greater insult for you to think that you could then leave the presence of your Master! Because somebody was a little rude to you, then you could be unpardonably rude to Christ.

Is there some Christian reader who, has realised, even as he follows this study, that his own Christian life has come to a halt? Your spiritual experience of salvation has been arrested; you are bogged down. You have come absolutely to a dead stop, because you fell out with somebody, or somebody insulted you, or was unkind to you, or forgot to thank you; or you were not put on a committee; you were criticized at the deacons' court; the Sunday School superintendent wasn't very appreciative. Because of a breakdown in relationships with other Christians you have come to this dead stop, and have not grown for weeks and months and years. Paul was very much concerned about this working out of Christian life to its completion, this continuing progress in the salvation of the soul.

'*Your own* salvation': there is something absolutely unique about the experience of grace that God is wanting to work in *you*. Your experience of Christ, your contribution to the church, is quite different from anyone else's. You have something to offer that nobody else can give. If you do not offer it, if your growth and development become arrested, the church is going to be so much the poorer. Work out your own salvation – work it out to the end. Never allow yourself to be halted, or stunted – you will be robbing the church.

Remember, too, it is God's work: your progress is God working in you, both initiating and seeking to fulfil. So Paul says, 'Do it with fear and trembling.' You and I should be terribly afraid! Afraid of what? – Of disappointing God. Can you remember playing in a tennis tournament, it may be, and you hoped so much that your father and mother would be among the spectators? Suddenly you spotted them! They had said they would be late; they were not sure of getting there in time, but they were there! And while you were so thrilled to see them, a sense of fear came immediately into the game. Just for a moment you started worrying.

What were you worrying about? The person on the other side of the net? No, you were worrying about the possibility of disappointing your parents. They were watching. You did not want to let them down, to hurt them, to disappoint them. You wanted to win, not for your own sake, but for their sakes! So you and I ought to be afraid of disappointing God; of hurting him. After all, he has done so much, at such a price.

'Work out your own salvation': work it out to

the end, to its fulness, to its completion, to its beauty, to its symmetry and balance, its completeness. Work it out to the *end*. Do not get halted; do not get stopped because some relationship has gone wrong. Aim constantly toward *continuing progress*.

Aim too for

(ii) *A convincing witness*

How closely Paul ties this up with our witness to the world. 'Do all things without murmurings and disputings; that ye may be blameless and harmless, the sons of God, without rebuke, in the midst of a crooked and perverse nation, among whom ye shine as lights in the world; holding forth the word of life; that I may rejoice' (2: 14–16).

'Do all things without murmurings.' Do not grizzle, winge, whimper, or fret! Do you know the kind of Christian who is very severe and grim; who very seldom smiles? If you see one at the women's meeting, or at the street corner, and see the heads going – *and* the tongues – you know perfectly well what they are talking about. They are having another good grizzle. Something has gone wrong. You know, the minister walked right past me in the street! Or, So-and-so sat right next to me and never spoke to me all the meeting through! You know the kind – the grizzlers. May we be delivered from grizzling, because it bears no witness and offers no testimony.

As we saw, this whole question of relationships is tied up very closely with

Christian witness. The world desperately wants
to know a solution to its manifold divisions, and
we need to be quite certain that we are offering
it. We have to be consistent, all the way
through.

I cannot help thinking that there are some
people today who feel that *not* to be one with
other Christians is almost a mark of greater
sanctity and greater Christlikeness; that you are
a better Christian if you do not have fellowship.
But you are *not* a better Christian if you are not
having fellowship with other born-again
Christians: you are a dishonouring Christian;
you are sinning against the unity of the Spirit.
The Spirit is one, and you are grieving the
Spirit. I am not saying necessarily that we are
all going to do everything all together, all the
time. As there is infinite variety in God's natural
creation, so there can be infinite variety in
God's spiritual creation; but there can be a basic
unity.

For example: there is something basically
wrong where a Christian man condemns one
section of the Christian Church in South Africa
because it will not allow into its fellowship, and
into its worship, a man whose skin happens to
be brown, and yet has no similar word of
condemnation of his own particular church that
will not allow a man to come to the Lord's table,
skin white and all, if he happens to be
Methodist or Baptist! The two attitudes just do
not tie up. When a man talks like that he gives
every appearance of being a humbug, however
sincere he may think he is. The two things just

do not make sense, and the world is watching.

How can we get over these barriers of relationship? People look to the church; they look to the Christian, and they get no answer. Where are they looking today? They are looking to Moscow. Make no mistake, if they look to Moscow, Moscow will respond and come to them. And it will not be the first time that God has taken something away from one privileged nation and given it to another – even if he does it in judgment. It is essential in these days that by harmonious Christian relationships the church shall maintain, beside a *continuing progress, a convincing witness,* that the world might believe.

Paul rounds off his persuasive argument with

4. THE SAMPLES DISPLAYED

I like to think that as Paul was writing of this potential problem, blended in his mind with the purpose of the letter, instinctively he thought of two men who illustrated perfectly what he was getting at: Timothy whom he was going to send forward to Philippi in a little while; and Epaphroditus who was now going back, having been a sick man. There are two things that he found in them which illustrate this kind of life of Christian relationship and this kind of love. First of all, in Timothy, Paul found

(i) *Unselfish concern*

'The kind of man who will genuinely care for your affairs' (2: 20). Are you, in the fellowship of

your church, the kind of Christian who
genuinely cares for the affairs of others? You are
not there just to be invited to sit in a group, or
to be thanked by the minister, or to be put on a
committee; you are there because you are
genuinely concerned about others.

Such was Timothy: in Epaphroditus Paul
found

(ii) *Unstinted service*

'He nearly died for the work of Christ,
hazarding his very life.' The physical effort and
exhaustion, the illness that dogged his footsteps
as he worked himself to the uttermost limits,
first in serving the Philippians and then in
serving Paul, brought his very life into danger.

There are places in the world, still, where
danger is part of the price of devotion. Such
physical danger may not be along our road, but
what about physical effort? Epaphroditus had
hazarded his very life; he was physically worn
out and exhausted; he had become ill; and all in
the service of Paul.

I remember helping somebody on with an
overcoat on a streaming wet Sunday night, and
saying 'I think you deserve a medal for coming
out on a night like this!' The rain was
thundering on the roof. She turned to me and
said, 'I won't get a medal when I go to work
tomorrow morning, even if it's as wet as it is
tonight.'

One thing that shocks and shames me is that
when it is a wet day, the average age of a
congregation leaps up. On a wet night we get

the old folk out who if anything have no business to be out; they already have rheumatism and it will be made worse. The folk who stay in, not prepared to go out because it is wet, are the lazy young folk.

Selfless concern for others. We want a few more Epaphrodituses knocking about – or Epaphroditi, if that is the correct plural of that particular name – folk who are prepared to be *exhausted* in unstinted service for Jesus Christ.

One thing both writer and readers *must* accept from this study of Philippians: if you and I are going to live a life sustained always by joy, it will have right at its heart a right relationship with other people. You will not be able to rejoice so long as you suffer dislocation, whether in your elbow, in your finger, or in your heart. *Get right with others – you will never sing until you do.*

FINALLY, my brethren, rejoice in the Lord. To write the same things to you, to me indeed *is* not grievous, but for you *it is* safe.

2 Beware of dogs, beware of evil workers, beware of the concision.

3 For we are the circumcision, which worship God in the spirit, and rejoice in Christ Jesus, and have no confidence in the flesh.

4 Though I might also have confidence in the flesh. If any other man thinketh that he hath whereof he might trust in the flesh, I more:

5 Circumcised the eighth day, of the stock of Israel, *of* the tribe of Benjamin, an Hebrew of the Hebrews; as touching the law, a Pharisee;

6 Concerning zeal, persecuting the church; touching the righteousness which is in the law, blameless.

7 But what things were gain to me, those I counted loss for Christ.

8 Yea doubtless, and I count all things *but* loss for the excellency of the knowledge of Christ Jesus my Lord: for whom I have suffered the loss of all things, and do count them *but* dung, that I may win Christ,

9 And be found in him, not having mine own righteousness, which is of the law, but that which is through the faith of Christ, the righteousness which is of God by faith:

10 That I may know him, and the power of his resurrection, and the fellowship of his sufferings, being made conformable unto his death;

11 If by any means I might attain unto the resurrection of the dead.

12 Not as though I had already attained, either were already perfect: but I follow after, if that I may apprehend that for which also I am apprehended of Christ Jesus.

13 Brethren, I count not myself to have apprehended: but *this* one thing *I do*, forgetting those things which are behind, and reaching forth unto those things which are before,

14 I press toward the mark for the prize of the high calling of God in Christ Jesus.

15 Let us therefore, as many as be perfect, be thus minded: and if in anything ye be otherwise minded, God shall reveal even this unto you.

16 Nevertheless, whereto we have already attained, let us walk by the same rule, let us mind the same thing.

17 Brethren, be followers together of me, and mark them which walk so as ye have us for an example.

18 (For many walk, of whom I have told you often, and now tell you even weeping, *that they are* the enemies of the cross of Christ:

19 Whose end *is* destruction, whose God *is their* belly, and *whose* glory *is* in their shame, who mind earthly things.)

20 For our conversation is in heaven; from whence also we look for the Saviour, the Lord Jesus Christ:

21 Who shall change our vile body, that it may be fashioned like unto his glorious body, according to the working whereby he is able even to subdue all things unto himself.

4

JOY – AND THE PERSON I AM

WE REACH our fourth study in the letter to
the Philippians, still seeking the secrets of
'the life of continual rejoicing'. We have
tried to detach it from its merely local and
historical setting to discover some of its spiritual
significance for our lives today.

After the introduction we came upon an intensely personal note – 'the things which happened unto *me*' – and realized that 'the place we
are in' has very often a great deal to do with our
ability or otherwise to rejoice. Then the atmosphere and emphasis changed, and we were
brought to face the theme of personal relationships – 'let your behaviour be as it becometh the
gospel of Christ'. The place we are in, the
people we are with: how often these constitute
our problems and militate against our joy.

When we come to chapter 3, the pendulum of
emphasis swings again, and Paul covers now
another area both of truth and of experience.

Here he is dealing, not with events or places, and not so much with people, but with the heart of personal religious experience. Chapter 3 has a very strong note of personal testimony running through it. Paul begins and ends by referring to others who have different views from his own; but the core and heart of the chapter deals with his own personal, spiritual experience.

I want to suggest that here we discover another factor we have to take into account when we are considering 'the life of continual rejoicing'. Our rejoicing is determined not only by the place we are in, not only by the people we may be with, but by the kind of Christians we are – *the person I am.*

One of the lessons we can learn from this particular section is that if we are going to be rejoicing Christians we each must be a *certain kind of Christian.* There are some Christians who will never be able to rejoice, while they remain at the standard of Christian experience they now know. Let us then get down to a closer study of this truth.

Once again we are going to take the whole passage, try to find strands of truth that hold together, and then see if we cannot define some principles of Christian living that will determine the measure of rejoicing that we as Christians may know. There are three words suggested by this chapter that it seems to me sum up Paul's attitude to himself as a Christian, Paul's attitude to the Christian experience, if you like, in its fulness. The first word is rather unexpected – it is the word

1. BANKRUPTCY

I have never been bankrupt yet, in the sense of having been to court about it; but I cannot imagine that bankruptcy in the complete sense is a very pleasant experience! But Paul suggests here that bankruptcy in the spiritual sense is one of the conditions of happiness! That is to say, if you are going to be a happy Christian you are going to be a bankrupt Christian, not of course in terms of cash, but in other terms altogether, as we shall discover.

This note of bankruptcy, of worthlessness, of emptiness, failure, comes in two sections, and I am going to pull in a third, with possibly just a touch of pressure, because to do so completes the picture and covers the whole chapter.

In verse 7, when Paul is recalling his pre-Christian life he describes all the rich heritage of religion that he enjoyed and experienced as a Jew, and he writes that off as dead loss. 'What things were gain to me, those I counted loss for Christ. Yea doubtless, and I still count them loss for the excellency of the knowledge of Christ Jesus my Lord.' He is looking back to his pre-Christian religious life, and he says that to him now it is worthless.

Paul then recalls the achievements of his career as a Christian. In verse 13 — and indeed he is beginning to look at it in verse 12: 'Not as though I had already attained, either were already perfect': — but in verse 13, 'Brethren, I count not myself to have apprehended' he again writes right across these — *worthless*. Finally in the closing section he refers to another kind of religious experience. In verses 18 and 19 I think we can understand the word 'walk', used so consistently by Paul of the Christian walk, to mean a professedly Christian experience, and a seemingly valid one. When Paul says 'For many walk, of whom I have told you often, and now tell you even weeping, that they are the enemies of the cross of Christ: whose end is destruction, whose God is their belly, whose glory is in their shame, who mind earthly things', he is speaking of people whose conduct reflected a trend of Christianity that was making a farce of the Christian gospel. They did this by living lives of licentious indulgence.

The first thought, then, in this section is one of bankruptcy. And after all, is this not a reflection, or a repetition, in more detail of the principle stated by our Lord: 'Happy, or blessed, are the poor in spirit, for theirs is the kingdom of heaven'? What Paul is getting at is, that if you and I are going to be really happy we must realize that we have *nothing* – apart from Christ, of course. In ourselves, in our pre-Christian tradition, in the long record of Christian achievement and experience that may be ours, in a way of life that can become a travesty of the gospel, we will never find happiness.

I am going to skim briefly over this first point about bankruptcy because it is not directly relevant to our life today, not in any immediate sense. Let us look at

(i) *A tradition that was rich* in Paul's pre-

Christian experience. Paul has remembered, for one reason or another, the party that dogged his footsteps everywhere, emerging at Rome in all probability, and at Philippi. This party said you could not be a Christian unless you were also a Jew; they insisted that if you were to be a Christian you must also undergo all the rites and regulations of the Jewish law. Paul begins his reply by stating how completely he was part of all that was best in the Jewish religion and race; but he adds that now, after coming upon God's revelation in Christ, he reckoned that in comparison it was all worthless, all part of his spiritual bankruptcy.

Part of this so rich tradition was a pure accident of birth. (Incidentally, is it not true that most of our denominationalism is an accident of birth too?) All his life long Paul had been a Jew, he was not a proselyte for he had been circumcised the eighth day. He was of the stock of Israel — that is to say, a pure Jew. There were other races that traced their lineage back to Abraham, but the pure Jew, the Israelite, traced his lineage back not only to Abraham but especially to Jacob, who was called Israel. He was a pure Jew. Further, he was of the tribe of Benjamin, the tribe that gave Israel their first king; that is to say, Paul belonged to the aristocracy of Israel.

But all this was an accident of birth — this very rich tradition of his. Added to it were his own personal achievements in the realm of religion and race. He was an Hebrew of the Hebrews — that is, his family was one that,

although living outside Palestine, not only spoke
Hebrew but maintained jealously in their lives
everything that was distinctively characteristic of
their own race. There were Jews who did not do
either of these; they adapted their way of life to
the customs, and they talked the language, of the
country of their adoption. Paul was not that
kind of Jew.

As touching the law he was a trained Pharisee,
highly educated and religious. Indeed, he was
not only deeply religious, he was fanatical. His
zeal was shown in the fact that he persecuted the
enemies of his race. If you asked anyone to
examine Paul's record concerning his fulfilment
of the countless requirements of the law, Paul
would be given full marks. A social and religious
aristocrat! And yet he says that when he came
across Christ, all *that* faded into insignificance;
it became so unimportant that for him it was
like a dung heap.

In the plan and provision of God in Christ he
had found the answer to the age-old dilemma of
the soul – How can a man be justified with God?
What he found in Christ was planned by God,
provided by God, perfected by God, and could
only be accepted by man as a gift from God;
and that gift made every other kind of heritage
insignificant. His was a tradition which was rich;
he now wrote it off as *worthless*.

But in addition, there had been in his experience as a Christian

(ii) *A triumph which was real*

Paul's Christian experience had been an amazing one. What a record Paul had of churches built, of journeys made, of men and women brought to Christ, of growing knowledge and understanding of the truth, of proving the faithfulness and the promises of God! And yet as Paul looked back down the years of his long Christian experience of wonderful service and great success, he said, 'I count not myself to have apprehended.' He says in effect, 'You know, when I look back along the way I have come, I feel as if I have hardly started; all I want to do concerning that which is behind me is to forget it. So I turn away from the things that are behind, and press on.'

I believe that here lies a very important element in the question of rejoicing. There is real danger that we rest upon the past; that we rely on what God did yesterday to satisfy us for today. We try to get the fun and sparkle of Christian experience while all the time we are living on stale grace. Once upon a time it *was* very wonderful, but it is not new.

Do you remember the manna experience of the children of Israel recorded in Exodus 16? In verse 20 we read of those who, having been told that they were to get their manna every morning – and they were to get it early because when the sun was up it would melt away – were lazy, and thought they would try to slip a fast one over God and over Moses. They would keep their manna from one day till the next. But we read that it 'bred worms and stank'.

I believe some Christians, too, lack a singing experience because they have a 'stinking' one!

It's so old that it smells! They are living on stale grace – if there can be such a thing. Their Christian experience is all old, all past, all done, all finished. And they are trying to drag along this stale grace, like stale cake, with them! No wonder they can't sing! A cake can be very lovely when it is fresh; I know of no lovelier household smell than that which used to greet me in Carlisle, where a lot of people still bake home bread. What a lovely fragrance it is when you come into the house! I like fresh cake and I like new bread – it may not be very good for you and certainly is not good for the figure, but it's very enjoyable. But I do *not* like stale cake, or stale bread. Is your Christian experience stale? I believe this to be one of the reasons why a lot of Christians are not rejoicing – they are spiritually stale, as stale as can be. There is nothing *new* about them anywhere. Yet they were called to 'walk in newness of life'!

There was no doubt that Paul's Christian experience had begun with *a triumph which was real*; its reality was proved no less by its constant repetition. It was a triumph continually renewed *in Christ*: but for that even his past triumphs would have been worthless.

Paul then deals with

(iii) *A travesty which was rife*

No joy is going to be found in the kind of experience of which Paul writes in verse 18 that 'many walk of whom I have told you often, and now tell you even weeping, that they are the enemies of the cross of Christ: whose end is destruction, whose god is their belly, and whose glory is in their shame'. He was thinking of the kind of Christian that possibly was emerging at Philippi and that he knew had emerged else-where, who had so twisted the gospel that they had been led into lives of indulgence and licen-tiousness, scandal and shame. These Christians were saying, 'It doesn't matter if we sin'; 'More sin, more grace'; 'We are no longer under law, so we can do as we like'.

We have to be fastidiously careful how we interpret that phrase in scripture – 'not under the law'. What does it mean? Does it mean that the law is no longer obligatory upon the Christian? Well, what does the New Testament say? Our Lord said, 'I came not to destroy the law but to fulfil it': – he came to make it not different but deeper in its meaning. What does Paul say? He says that the sum total of God's working in our lives is in order that *the righteousness of the law might be fulfilled in us*.

Of course we are not under the law so far as *getting right* with God is concerned: we can never *get* right with God through the law. Grace has taken the place of law so far as getting right with God is concerned. But so far as *being* right with God is concerned, the law remains. 'Thou shalt not steal.' Has that nothing to do with the Christian? Of course it has. No, we are not under the law so far as getting right with God is concerned, neither are we under the Jewish ceremonial law.

But if Christ said, 'I came not to destroy but to fulfil', have we any business to destroy? I

have come across Christians who take this attitude that the law does not matter, and what
immediately happens? If the law does not matter, sin does not matter. It is by the law that the
knowledge of sin comes. 'Sin is the transgression
of the law.' And that is true of sin in the life of
the Christian.

Some Christians seem to have almost no ethi-
cal standards at all. In business, some of the
biggest twisters are Christians. On Sunday they
will stand up and preach the gospel, and on
Monday they go off and trick and deceive an
unconverted businessman. Is it any wonder that
sometimes when I have been talking to utterly
worldly and ungodly men about the things of
Christ, they say, 'Oh yes, I know all that. But
then I happen to know what these men are like
in business. I have known them do things in
business that I, a man who never goes to
church, would not stoop to do!' If the law does
not matter, sin does not matter; that is what these
licentious Christians were saying, and in con-
sequence they were living lives of utter lawless-
ness and indulgence.

Paul says, 'You won't find joy in that kind of
spiritual experience. Do you know what you
really are? You are an enemy of the cross.'
These people who were glorying in the cross
said, 'Oh, now there's grace, there's mercy, pardon, forgiveness'; to them Paul said, 'You who
are glorying in the cross and living like that, you
are the *enemies* of the cross.' And that, too, is
bankruptcy!

There is no joy along any of these lines; no

joy if we are resting on a tradition which may be
very rich, but which is outside of Christ; no joy
if we are resting on a triumph which is real, but
which is past; no joy if our Christianity contains
this travesty of the gospel, which in Paul's day
was so rife and which really was blasphemy so
far as the cross was concerned. Along these
lines, there is certainly no joy, only negation,
and spiritual insolvency.

But notice now what Paul has to say positively
about

2. INTIMACY

Here we move right on to the predominant
theme of chapter 3. The whole atmosphere of
this wonderful testimony is the intimacy of our
communion with Christ. Verse 10 is the key
'That I may know him and the power of his
resurrection, and the fellowship of his sufferings, being made conformable unto his death.'
That word translated 'know' is not the 'know' of
the intellect; it is the 'know' of intimacy. The
Scottish language has a delightful phrase to
describe friendship which is on such terms of
rare intimacy. It is the phrase 'far ben' based on
the old country set-up when a cottage would
have two rooms, a but and a ben. The 'but' was
the room that everybody went into; the 'ben'
was the room into which you took only those
you peculiarly wished to honour! And that word
became transferred from ordinary life to friendship; if you were on privileged terms of

intimate friendship with someone who rejoiced
in your friendship, you were described as being
'far ben' with such a person.

Does anybody remember the books of Ian
Maclaren – now out of print, and I dare say out
of date in the minds of many people – stories of
the Drumtochty folk, *The Days of Auld Lang
Syne*, *Beside the Bonnie Briar Bush* and others?
If so, you may recall how in one story Ian
Maclaren describes the village folk gossiping
around the walls of the kirkyard, talking about
one and another as country folk do! When they
had discussed almost everybody, someone mentioned the name of one man who was quite
outstanding for sheer Christian worth and character. 'What do you think of Burnbrae?'

At the mention of the name silence fell; it was
not easy to do justice to such a man. 'Well, there
is only one thing you can say about Burnbrae
and that is, he is "far ben".' Burnbrae was 'far
ben' with God; that is what Paul wanted to be
with Jesus Christ – 'That I may know him and
the power of his resurrection, and the fellowship
of his sufferings.'

Paul wanted to know, for one thing

(i) *The Person of his Lord*

Here is the goal of all Christian endeavour, of
all Christian experience. The first thing, the all-
important thing, is to know Christ.

How many of us get things out of order!
Sometimes we put power first; sometimes we
put blessing first; sometimes success, sometimes
the blessing of the fulness of the Spirit. If we put

any one of these first we are wrong. 'That I may know *him*'. When our Lord chose the twelve, he chose them that they might be '*with him*'. This is a corrective we can apply to much of our thinking, to much of our praying.

I remember how, as a young fellow growing up in Christian work through adolescence, the great cry of my heart was for power. Is anyone reading this of whom the same is true? – you would give anything to have power; power in your own life, power in your Christian service. So it was with me. Then one day, with no preacher present to instruct me but simply with my Bible open in front of me, I read through Philippians 3: 10 and I suddenly saw that I was wrong in wanting power first! There was something that mattered much more, that should come before power, and that was the person of my Lord ... 'that I might know him'. So I gave myself to this matter first. If you have your spiritual priorities out of order, get them straightened out, put Christ first. 'That I may know him' – that is what matters.

Incidentally, this would help many as a corrective in their thinking about the Holy Spirit. I have never forgotten some words of the Principal at my Theological College. He was a very deeply-taught Bible student, and a very sane and godly Christian man. He was speaking to us as young theological students, with all our enthusiasm and all that lack of balance which is the mark of youth. It cannot be easy when you are a Principal of a Bible or Theological College, trying to keep under control a lot of young men

as restive and as undisciplined as wild horses.
There are movements that sometimes pass
through such a college. There were among us
men who were longing for the baptism of the Holy
Spirit, as they called it. Others sought the
fulness of the Holy Spirit. Still others sought for
the second, third or fourth blessing. There were
all sorts of ambitions.

But I remember the Principal saying to us
something like this: 'You can always test any
claimed blessing of the Holy Spirit in one way,
and if it doesn't meet this test it is not a valid
experience, however it is described or defined,
and whether or not you use the language of
Scripture: there is one valid test of any experience of the Holy Spirit: *Does it bring me to a
deeper knowledge of Christ?*' If it does not bring
me to a deeper knowledge of Christ, it is not the
work of the Spirit of God. Why? Because we
read of that very same Holy Spirit, '*He* shall
testify of *me*'. '*He* shall glorify *me*.' Christ said
that of the Spirit of God. What matters is not –
Am I excited? Am I moved? But – Do I know
Christ more? If you do not know Christ more
after a so-called experience of the Spirit of God,
then question the validity of that experience
right away. Paul wanted 'to know him' – the
person of his Lord.

But Paul wanted to know, secondly, concerning
Christ

(ii) *The Power of His life*

Or, as verse 10 has it, 'the power of his
resurrection'. This is not just the power that

raised him, but the power that marked the quality of life that our Lord entered into through his resurrection. That risen life had a quality of power about it that Paul wanted to know. It was a life which lay on the further side of the cross, a life which Romans 6 describes as being 'dead *unto* sin'.

When you look at the life of our Lord before and after the cross, can you tell me one thing missing on the resurrection side which is far from missing on the pre-Calvary side? I am not being dogmatic here: all I am doing is asking you to think this out. Before the cross, our Lord was tempted in all points like as we are; and the battle of temptation raged fiercely and ceaselessly right up to the very moment of death, with the final temptation, 'If thou be the Son of God come down from the cross'. Is there any temptation after the cross? None. The battle is over. The victory is won. When our Lord on the cross gave voice to that shout of triumph 'It is finished', was it simply because the work of atonement was complete? I wonder. I sometimes wonder if that was *not* just a shout of victory concerning the work, but also a sob of thankfulness from the Warrior who had finished the battle!

I am not saying that when you and I enter into the experience of the resurrection life of our Lord, temptation ceases. I am not saying that for one moment. But I do want to suggest that there is, in the risen life of our Lord, a *quality* which, if we like to use it, and to grasp its fullest meaning, is a life which has entered into

an immunity against which temptation is futile;
an immunity from which temptation falls back
like broken waves beating against a massive rock.

Our Lord lived his tempted life all the way
through, and having proved victorious over
every temptation, he brought that victory with
him through the cross and into the resurrection
life. That is the victory which becomes ours
when we share the power of resurrection life
with him.

I remember years ago hearing the Rev. L. F.
E. Wilkinson say that he had heard of a
Frenchman who became an Englishman because
he so admired our British way of life. He had
lived in England so long that he decided to take
out 'naturalisation' papers and become an
Englishman. Someone asked him what difference it made: 'Well,' he said, 'among other
things I find that now, instead of losing the
battle of Waterloo, I've won it!' He had stepped
into the heritage of all that Britain had fought
for, and all that Britain had won, and it was now
his. When you and I step into Christ we step
into resurrection life; all that Christ has achieved
and all that Christ has won becomes ours – if we
care to use it.

And then, thirdly, Paul desired to know not
only *the person of his Lord* and *the power of his
life*, but also

(iii) *The Passion of his love*

'That I may know him and the power of his
resurrection and the fellowship of his sufferings.' This verse is rather like a jam sandwich:

the jam is in the middle – 'the power of his resurrection'. I want the jam, but the discipline of getting to know him is a different matter! I do not know that I am quite so keen about that; and as for sharing the fellowship of his sufferings, I do not know whether I am interested in that at all! But when you take a sandwich you do not scoop out the jam; you bite through the whole sandwich. 'That I may know him' – the Person of my Lord. 'That I may know the power of his resurrection' – the power of his life. 'That I may know ... the fellowship of his sufferings' – that I may know the passion of my Lord's love.

What did this mean – the fellowship of the sufferings of Christ? What was his suffering, primarily? Surely it was the bearing of the sin of the world. You and I will never come to know him unless we get under the burden of the world's need. That is why some Christians do not know Christ as they should. It is not that they do not know their Bible: they know their Bible all right. But they do not fully know their Lord. Why? Because they have never known him in the fellowship of his sufferings.

How many readers will know those slightly sentimental and romantic novels of Grace Richmond? Her chief character was a doctor called Red Pepper, because he had red hair: Red Pepper Burns. On one occasion, Red Pepper was about to go out to conduct an operation, and his assistant and secretary, who worked very closely with him, was busy getting things ready. Then Red Pepper, glancing up, suddenly caught a

look in the eyes of his wife. At that moment it
dawned on him that his wife envied this girl,
this nurse and secretary. Desperately she envied
her going out and working with her husband
during this operation. So he said, 'Do you want
to come?' And she replied, 'I'd give anything to
come.' And so she went.

You see, a surgeon may not be really known
by his wife. She knows him as a surgeon-at-
home; she knows him as a man. But he is more
than a man; he is more than a surgeon-at-home;
he is a surgeon in the operating theatre. His wife
never knows him there, unless she works with
him there, like the sister in charge, or a nurse.
They know him.

You can never know Christ until you work
with him, until you get under the burden of the
world's need, and become, like our Lord, one
upon whom is laid the sin of the world. Not in
atonement – he did that uniquely; but in the
continuing work of redemption.

Paul said, 'I want to know him – the Person
of my Lord; I want to know the power of his
resurrection – the quality of life that is now his,
and mine through him; but I want to know also
the passion of his love.' Only such *intimacy* with
Christ could fully absolve Paul's spiritual
bankruptcy.

The third word, suggested by this chapter, that
helps to define Paul's attitude to Christian life is

3. EXPECTANCY

If stale cake is dull, new cake is always

exciting. There is something lovely about a new
thing. Ladies love to buy new clothes, a new
spring costume, or a winter suit or coat; men are
different in this. But with some Christians,
expectancy of new things just is not there! It
was there with Paul. There was always a beyond, always something new. That was another
reason why he was always rejoicing. In this
expectancy there were three elements that played
their parts. There was

(i) *The Voice that calls*

Paul describes it here – and I am translating it
rather as Handley Moule does – as the summons
from the heights, the voice of God. That was
what mattered in the heart of this man. The
voices of his Christian friends did not matter;
the voice of his own self did not matter: the one
voice that mattered was the summons from the
heights, the high calling of God. From the
heights! That speaks of climbing, and of effort.
'Does the road wind uphill all the way? Yes, to
the very end.' *The Voice that calls.*

The second element in Paul's expectancy was

(ii) *The Vision that counts*

'I follow after, if that I may apprehend that
for which I am apprehended of Christ Jesus' (v.
12). The thing that mattered supremely in
Paul's life was to fulfil the destiny that was for
him in Christ.

Every mother has a dream for her child, every
father a dream for his son. And Christ had a
dream for Paul. Paul says, 'I want to fulfil the

dream. I was apprehended by Christ for a
special purpose, for a special task, and I'm going
to go on, and on, and on, until that dream is
fulfilled.'

And the third element in Paul's expectancy
was his anticipation of

(iii) *The Verdict that crowns*

What is the one thing that will ultimately
matter? What is the prize for which Paul is
striving, this final thing which is our great
reward? Surely it is that the Master will say to
the servant who has pursued so long and travelled so far, 'Well done!' That will be the verdict
that crowns.

My father was a great cricketer. Often he
would recall his cricketing days, as captain of
the school, captain of the University for three
years. He used to say that what really thrilled
him during his cricketing career was not when
he had knocked up another century and was
coming into the pavilion amid the applause of
the spectators; it was not when he took another
wicket. The great thrill to him was when he
went round to see his father, and as he went into
the room his old father would say, 'Well, how
have you got on today, John?' then – O the joy
when he was able to tell his father that he had
done well, and heard his father's 'Well done!'

The verdict that crowns will be this – when
you and I get home and we are able to go in and
tell the Father that we have done well, and to
hear him say, 'Well done!' That forward look of
Paul, that expectant look which reached right on

to the verdict, to the prize-giving day, brought heaven into view!

The moment heaven came into view, Paul realized that although it might be that he would go there to receive the prize, it might also be that the Master might come here. So his expectancy was further quickened by the thought of the possible return of Christ; and as he ends this section of his letter Paul remembers that from thence, from heaven itself, will come the Saviour for whom we look. So it is not a remote expectancy – remote because the prize-giving day is far off; that day may come any time now. Surely the coming of the Lord draweth near! And in that expectancy we live, 'for every man that hath this hope purifieth himself even as he is pure'.

I want to end by quoting three verses of a lovely poem that Mr Hudson Pope gave to us at Keswick at family prayers in the Speakers' House. It is called 'Supposing he came tonight'. He got it from a notebook that he found among his wife's possessions after she had gone home.

> My work for the day is almost through;
> Was it all as in his sight?
> Would Jesus be able to say, 'Well done!'
> Supposing he came tonight?
>
> There's a tiny sin on my soul today,
> And I can't make my face look bright.
> Would Jesus ask, 'Aren't you glad I've come?'
> Supposing he came tonight?
>
> Lord Jesus, I want more grace each day,
> To help me to walk aright,
> So that my heart may welcome you
> Supposing you came tonight.

A Prayer:
Oh, may we stand before the Lamb
  When earth and seas are fled,
And hear the Judge pronounce our name
  With blessings on our head.

THEREFORE, my brethren dearly beloved and longed for, my joy and crown, so stand fast in the Lord, *my* dearly beloved.

2 I beseech Euodias, and beseech Syntyche, that they be of the same mind in the Lord.

3 And I intreat thee also, true yokefellow, help those women which laboured with me in the gospel, with Clement also, and *with* other my fellowlabourers, whose names *are* in the book of life.

4 Rejoice in the Lord alway: *and* again I say, Rejoice.

5 Let your moderation be known unto all men. The Lord *is* at hand.

6 Be careful for nothing; but in every thing by prayer and supplication with thanksgiving let your requests be made known unto God.

7 And the peace of God, which passeth all understanding, shall keep your hearts and minds through Christ Jesus.

8 Finally, brethren, whatsoever things are true, whatsoever things *are* honest, whatsoever things *are* just, whatsoever things *are* pure, whatsoever things *are* lovely, whatsoever things *are* of good report; if *there be* any virtue, and if *there be* any praise, think on these things.

9 Those things, which ye have both learned, and received, and heard, and seen in me, do: and the God of peace shall be with you.

10 But I rejoiced in the Lord greatly, that now at the last your care of me hath flourished again; wherein ye were also careful, but ye lacked opportunity.

11 Not that I speak in respect of want: for I have learned, in whatsoever state I am, *therewith* to be content.

12 I know both how to be abased, and I know how to abound: every where and in all things I am instructed both to be full and to be hungry, both to abound and to suffer need.

13 I can do all things through Christ which strengtheneth me.

14 Notwithstanding ye have well done, that ye did communicate with my affliction.

15 Now ye Philippians know also, that in the beginning of the gospel, when I departed from Macedonia, no church communicated with me as concerning giving and receiving, but ye only.

16 For even in Thessalonica ye sent once and again unto my necessity.

17 Not because I desire a gift: but I desire fruit that may abound to your account.

18 But I have all, and abound: I am full, having received of Epaphroditus the things *which were sent* from you, an odour of a sweet smell, a sacrifice acceptable, well pleasing to God.

19 But my God shall supply all your need according to his riches in glory by Christ Jesus.

20 Now unto God and our Father *be* glory for ever and ever. Amen.

21 Salute every saint in Christ Jesus. The brethren which are with me greet you.

22 All the saints salute you, chiefly they that are of Caesar's household.

23 The grace of our Lord Jesus Christ *be* with you all. Amen.

5

THE CONCLUSION OF THE LETTER

THE FINAL STUDY in this Epistle of Joy, chapter 4, I am calling simply 'The Conclusion'. At the beginning of chapter 3 the word 'finally' occurred, before some unexpected thought had sent Paul's mind dancing along other lines. If any preacher wants scriptural authority for a very long 'finally' he has it in this Epistle! It could be maintained that the whole of chapter 3 was an unexpected, and originally unintended, utterance, a line of thought that came to Paul suddenly. It may be that somebody dropped in during the dictation, or before Paul picked up the letter again after a rest; it looks as though some such thing happened to send him off into that wonderful passage.

We would not have missed it for anything. If it did result from an interruption, then we can learn something from that fact; when we are interrupted sometimes, let us remember that an

interruption can potentially be an opportunity for
God. So do not get worked up and do not get
irritated if you are interrupted. It is possible
that we would never have had the third chapter
of 'Philippians' if Paul had not accepted an
interruption and turned it into an opportunity.

Following this digression in chapter 3, Paul
now comes to his final comments, greetings and
remarks. I want to take this chapter, which on
the face of it seems a little disjointed, and try to
find some cohesion that will unify the whole
passage. I think we can divide it into three
sections. First, verses 1–9 where Paul is dealing
with a specific problem in the Church at
Philippi. Then, verses 10–19 where he is dealing
with quite a different matter, and the whole
tenor of the letter is once again one of warmth
and affection. The Philippians had sent an
extremely generous offering not only in money
but also in service by Epaphroditus, and Paul's
heart is glowing as he thinks of their care of
him. And then we have the final salutation, in
verses 20–23. So we may divide the chapter
thus:

THE CONCERN IN HIS MIND (vv. 1–9)
THE CONTENT IN HIS HEART (vv. 10–
   19)
   THE CONCLUSION OF HIS LETTER
   (vv. 20–23)

1. THE CONCERN IN HIS MIND

There   was   one   thing   at   Philippi   that

occasioned concern for Paul. It was a lovely church, as we have seen, and although there were dangers emerging within it and surrounding it, Paul's whole attitude was one of warmth, affection, rejoicing and thanksgiving, except for one thing. This concern in his mind he must deal with before he closes the letter. He cannot allow the letter to run through to the end without raising it.

In verse 2 he pinpoints the matter that is worrying him. So we have there

(i) *The problem raised*

Euodias and Syntyche, two women who had worked with Paul, were apparently not on speaking terms. It is interesting to note that thus early women were making their vital contribution to the life of the church. We might do well to pause and consider what the church would do today without the faithfulness of its womenfolk. I wonder how many would be at the prayer meeting in your church if there were only men there! I wonder how many would be staffing our mission stations if there were only men! I sometimes think we men of the church should be utterly ashamed of ourselves for the way we leave so much of the work to the women.

I believe that one of the rules for a Rotarian is that he must attend the weekly lunch wherever he is. He must find out where the Rotary lunch is being held, in whatever town he happens to be that day, and he must be there. Men accept a rule like that in the realm of social friendliness and benevolence. Can Christian men not equally accept this kind of discipline, making it their rule to be at a prayer meeting every week? Deacons, Elders, Churchwardens, Lay preachers, Bible class leaders, Sunday school teachers, are you at your prayer meeting – or do you leave it to the women? One of the wonderful things about most women in the church is that when they are asked to do a thing they do it extremely well! There are some churches where, the moment there is anything extra to be tackled, those in authority say, 'Oh well, we'll ask the Women's Guild to do that.' Why do they ask the Guild or the Mothers' Union, or the Women's meeting? Because they know it will be done!

But here in this church things were far from well! I want to note *the prominence of the people* involved. They are described as those who had laboured with Paul. I do not think these were just of the rank and file of the church; they were people of some prominence: but they were not on speaking terms. They were not 'of the same mind' in the Lord. Some serious difference had occurred between them. It was causing trouble and anxiety in the church, and Paul says it must be dealt with.

Not only should we note the prominence of the people, but also *the persistence of the problem*. I wonder if this is suggested by verse 5 ... 'Let your moderation ...'. The meaning of that word, as Handley Moule suggests in his commentary, is 'let your *yieldingness* be known unto all men'. The fact that you are disagreeing is widely known, but let your yieldingness, the fact that you are willing to give way, are willing to be gracious – let that be known too, unto all men. The very fact that Paul seems to be suggesting that there was a lack of yieldingness implies that the situation had existed for some considerable time – hence the persistence of this problem as well as the prominence of the people involved.

Strange it is, and how inconsistent, about Christian living at executive level, that sometimes Christians who are in high office are out of fellowship with each other. The fact gets very widely known just because they are so prominent. Stranger it is that such a situation can go on year after year! There is a cautionary thought here for some of us. We must avoid assuming that the facts that we are growing up in our responsibilities in the church, and that God is using us, mean that we are getting beyond the need of correction. Those of us who are instructing others, or holding responsible office, are so accustomed to telling other people what they ought to do that we seldom stop to think that we might need to be told what we ought to do. Paul said, so far as this church was concerned, 'there are two prominent workers in the church; they are not on speaking terms; the matter must be dealt with.' It is possible, you know, to become even a Convention speaker and to think that because of this you are outside the range of God's corrective truth. Not a bit of it!

The problem once raised, we have also

(ii) *The Presence recalled*

'The Lord is at hand' (v. 5). That does not
refer to the coming of the Lord: I think that is
quite definite. The real meaning here is that 'the
Lord is near'. That is to say, Here is a church
where a certain situation has arisen, it has gone
on for a considerable time, it is no doubt the
topic of conversation in many homes and on
many lips; Paul says not only is there a problem
in your church, do not forget there is a
Presence. *The Lord* is near.

'Be careful for nothing: but in everything by
prayer and supplication with thanksgiving let
your requests be made known unto God' (v. 6).
In all your arguments, in all your self-
justification, in all your Christian gossip,
remember 'the Lord is near'. When you move
away from that difficult Deacons' Court, that
Committee meeting, and you stand at the street
corner, or sit in your car and talk for a little
while, remember that although there are only
two of you talking, there is a Third present. It is
in this context that Paul stresses *the value of
prayer*. If you and I prayed more about this
kind of problem and talked less, I wonder if we
would get to a quicker and simpler solution?
Paul, I think, is talking about prayer in the
context of this problem, but of course not
confining his thought to it.

I hope those readers who are younger
Christians have realized that prayer is not just
saying your prayers. Prayer is not merely
something you do by your bedside in the
morning, or at night, when the door is shut and

your eyes are shut. Of course prayer is something that you do then and there; but prayer is *talking to the Lord*. The Lord is at hand, the Lord is near, the Lord is at your elbow – well, *talk* to him then. And not just about a problem like this in the church, but about any problem.

If you lose something in the morning, you men, do not start shouting at your wife! Never get the whole house in a ferment because you cannot find the thing! Nor rush about getting increasingly irritated, saying 'Where did I put it? Where did I put it?' until everybody is looking for it! If you find you have mislaid something, say to yourself, 'Now Lord, where did I put it?' And then start looking for it, with the Lord.

You ladies, when your husband brings someone home for a meal unexpectedly, try not to get in a flap and go raging off into the kitchen saying, 'He might have told me he was going to bring So-and-so today. Doesn't he know I wasn't expecting anybody and that there is nothing in the bread bin and there is nothing in the cake tin; what does he expect?' Why not go off to the kitchen saying 'Now Lord, here's a pretty kettle of fish! What are we going to do about it? There is one thing, Lord, I could do that I am afraid I have not done this time. I could see that I always have something in reserve hidden away in the larder for just such an occasion. Sorry I haven't got it today, Lord, but I will try to remember to keep something always by me for an emergency.' So you go chatting it all over with the Lord. And do you know, *that* is prayer!

Was it C. T. Studd who said once in his room at Cambridge, rather startling his hearers, for he was a great cricketer, 'You know, when I play cricket, I don't think I play fair'? And they said, 'Why?' And he said, 'Because when I play I pray.' For C. T. Studd 'the Lord was at hand'.

In that church at Philippi there was a problem, a difficulty of relationship, and it was becoming common talk. Would it not have become less common talk among the members, if it had been more common talk with the Lord? Suppose that, instead of the Christians getting together and talking about it among themselves, they had just talked it over with the Lord: 'You know, Lord, these two, they are still not on speaking terms: I do wish they'd hurry up and put it right, Lord.' Talk to the Lord like that about this kind of problem, instead of getting down to a good quarter-of-an-hour's gossip on the street corner with So-and-so, and then stopping when you see one of the ladies concerned coming along, saying to your fellow gossip, 'Ssh! Here she is!'

But Paul also stresses *the virtue of praise*. Not only does he say that we have to pray about everything, he says we have to let praise come in too! What a corrective praise would have been to their prayers! They could have praised him because they knew that he would bring good out of it. They could have praised him because they knew that he would answer prayer. They could have praised him because of the service these folk had done in the past, to which they knew God would restore them. So let all our praying be coloured with praise. In such ways is *the Presence recalled*.

The problem being raised, and the Lord's presence being recalled, Paul now draws attention to

(iii) *The Practice recommended*

Verse 8 seems to be related to the same kind of problem that Paul has mentioned in verse 2. Paul is not only spiritual but sensible. (Some people are very spiritual but completely lacking in common sense!) So Paul becomes intensely practical: he says, 'This whole situation won't be resolved even by prayer, unless you stop thinking the nasty kind of thoughts you can so easily think.'

He is speaking here of the tremendous importance of the thought-life. He says, 'And so, brethren, whatsoever things are *true*, whatsoever things are *honest*, whatsoever things are *just*, whatsoever things are *pure*, whatsoever things are *lovely*, whatsoever things are of *good report*, keep thinking on these things.' Do not let your thought-life become a kind of gossip shop. There are some Christians who even if they do not gossip to another will gossip to themselves. They will allow all unkind, and sometimes untrue, unfair, impure, and unclean thoughts, to circulate in their minds.

The thought-life is tremendously important, not just in this context, but in every aspect of Christian work. If you are thinking unkindly of a person, or in an unfriendly way, that inner attitude which has become the constant habit in your mind, is something they are bound to sense whenever you meet them.

This is relevant to what we call personal work and soul-winning work. The average Christian can be very zealous, very keen, and sometimes what he would call very faithful, in trying to reach the unconverted. But his efforts are doomed before he begins if his whole attitude of mind to unconverted people is a critical one. 'They don't go to church; isn't it terrible? They never read their Bible; I think that's frightful. They live a kind of life that is absolutely godless; I think it's appalling.' Then you come to this person who you think is dreadful, frightful and appalling, and you try to win him for Christ! But he knows instinctively, the moment he meets you, that you think he is dreadful. So of course you never get anywhere with him.

I remember dear old Bishop Taylor Smith telling me once: 'When I meet a person I have never met before, and maybe feel in my heart I must bear some sort of witness or testimony, I don't assume that he is unconverted. I assume that he is in agreement with my outlook! I may find out in a matter of minutes that he isn't; but when I meet him I assume that he agrees with me. That means that in my mind I am not approaching him critically or censoriously. I am approaching him with an attitude which is friendly. We are at ease with one another right away.' We do well to follow the Bishop here, and to remember that our Lord was called the *friend* of sinners, not their critic.

Never get into the habit of going about saying So-and-so is unconverted – until you have found out and are quite sure. Do not even go up to a person assuming he is unconverted. If you are going to get really close to him, assume that he is a Christian. Of course you may find out very soon that he is not: in that case you will know how to deal with him; all is perfectly natural.

In this situation in the church, in this problem that is on his mind, Paul realized not only that the people should know they were involved in it, not only that prayer should be offered about it, but that the real sphere of the battle was in the mind and in the thought-life of the community. So he says, 'Keep thinking on things that have virtue in them, that have praise in them, and things that are of good report. Keep thinking on these things.'

Suppose Paul were to write a letter to your church, having a concern in his mind about your church because of a true report that had reached him: may I ask this question? The names in this letter are Euodias and Syntyche; but if Paul were writing to your church, would your name be in his letter? Are you a person involved in such a problem in your church right now? Well, Paul says, 'I want the problem dealt with.' And you know, I think the Lord wants to deal with it too.

2. THE CONTENT IN HIS HEART

Having dealt with the concern in his mind,
Paul returns to the warmth and affection and
love that generally mark the letter. Look at
verses 10 and 18: 'I rejoiced in the Lord greatly,
that now at the last your care of me hath
flourished again ... But I have all and abound:
I am full, having received of Epaphroditus the
things which were sent from you.'

Here is

V10
V14 — 18

(i) *A ministry they had shown*

'Your care of me hath flourished again.' I
want you to note the measure of it: their
generosity was an overflowing one. Paul says,
'You know you have sent far too much. I have
all and am just overflowing with it. I am full.' I
wonder how many missionaries can write home
and say, 'Thank you so much for my allowance.
You have sent me far too much!'

The Christian church in Great Britain has to
take the whole question of its giving much more
seriously. Do not let us be deceived by financial
statements, issued by some missionary societies,
which show no deficit. There are some
missionary societies that make it a policy never
to go into debt; and they are able to say, with a
measure of truth, that they have never done so.
Year after year their annual statement of
accounts is issued and there is no deficit shown
on paper. But I believe there is not infrequently
a grave deficit. It is not on paper at home. It is
in the purses of the missionaries on the field.

There is almost always a debt! It is not a debt owed to a business company or a trading concern at home, but it is a debt that is owed by the church at home to the missionaries on the field. Let us be a little bit more careful about this question of no deficit, no debt. It can deceive the church at home into thinking that everything is all right, whereas out on the field the missionaries, who are absolutely at their wits' end to know how to make ends meet, know that it is all wrong.

Paul says, 'You know, you have sent me far too much.' What is the measure of our giving today? The Church of Scotland, for instance, in 1960 asked of its membership for giving to missionary work the vast and sacrificial sum of five shillings (now twenty-five pence) in a year! That is the amount that children on holiday at that time would spend on ice cream in a week. Was that a fitting standard of generosity for the church to show in the missionary task?

I remember travelling with a Communist on the night train from Glasgow to London. He had been a Communist for thirty years. We had a long talk. I told him how in my world travels I had come to the conclusion that, although I had been brought up in the tradition that Britain could do no wrong, nevertheless we had not taken our Empire very seriously at all; now that we were beginning to do so, it was almost too late. He agreed with me that possibly the Christian concept of missionary work and hospitals and education appealed to him as a

Communist more than any other aspect of the
life of the church.

Having told him my own conviction, that
what we were doing was far from adequate, I
turned to him and said, 'What about the Labour
movement, the Trade Union movement? They
exist to look after the well-being and to care for
the interests of the worker. How much concern
does the Trade Union movement in this country
have in the well-being of what we called the
backward, the under-developed countries?'

He said, 'It is interesting you should raise
that; because my specific task at this time in the
Trade Union movement is to raise a levy from
every member of every Trade Union, to be used
for the well-being of the working class in under-
developed countries.' I said, 'How much is your
levy?' He said, 'One and sixpence' (now, seven
and a half pence). I said 'One and sixpence per
annum! That's not quite so good as the church
at five shillings per annum; I thought the church
was bad enough!' 'Oh,' he said, 'it's not one and
sixpence per annum; that levy has to be spread
over two years.'

If such giving truly reflects our concern, then
it indicates practically no concern at all. Let's
face it! In contrast, the generosity of the church
at Philippi thrilled Paul because it came as
evidence of their love, and because its fragrance
gave pleasure to God. But then, having mentioned their ministry, Paul offers

(ii) *A testimony he could give* ✓ 11 — 13
He says, 'You know, it's lovely of you to send

this, but I do want to bear my testimony that I have learned in all the vicissitudes of life, whether I have had a little or a lot, whether I have been at starvation level or whether I have been overwhelmed with generosity, I have learned in all the vicissitudes of life to be content. And I have discovered that I can cope with any situation through Christ who makes me strong' (vv. 11–13). I do not know which is more difficult – to have too little or to have too much. We need the grace of God to handle each situation.

So Paul ends. First of all he speaks in this section, where the content in his heart is so warm, of *a ministry they had shown;* then of *a testimony he could give;* and now of

(iii) *A sufficiency they would prove* 19

'But my God shall supply all your need according to his riches in glory by Christ Jesus' (v. 19).

And so, finally, having shared the concern in his mind, and expressed the content in his heart, Paul reaches

3. THE CONCLUSION OF HIS LETTER

'Now unto God and our Father be glory for ever and ever, Amen. Salute every saint in Christ Jesus. The brethren which are with me greet you. All the saints salute you, chiefly they that are of Caesar's household. The grace of our Lord Jesus Christ be with you all. Amen' (vv. 20–23).

First, as I pondered over the conclusion here,

(i) *The existence of the letter spoke to me*. The
fact is, there was a letter; we have been studying
it. Look back at the middle of verse 15, 'no church
communicated with me'. The reference there
may be financial and practical, but let us apply
it rather more widely. When did you last write
to a missionary? Have you one who has gone out
from your church into Christian work elsewhere
who looks longingly for a letter from home?

I had a letter the other day from a missionary.
He had received a letter from home which
referred to an address I had given at the Baptist
Missionary Society's service in Westminster
Chapel, when I raised this very point about
writing to missionaries. This young worker, out
on his first term for over a year, if not two
years, wrote 'Before I went out, at my farewell
meeting, my church people promised they would
write to me. But I haven't had a single letter
either from my pastor or the people.' Not a
single letter!

These missionaries come home and we
welcome them back; they stand up in our
churches and say, 'The first thing I want to do
is to thank you for remembering me.' I wonder
if they say it almost with a sob? They have to
say it, but in the desperate loneliness of the
mission field they often wondered if anyone was
remembering them! There was no tangible
evidence of it.

I get prayer letters from a number of
missionaries. We cannot be in touch with every

missionary: God will give you a selective ministry of responsibility here, as in other spheres of Christian work. But I find the best thing to do the moment a prayer letter comes in is to send at least a postcard out. Is there someone you know on the field to whom you have not written for months? Take five minutes now and send a postcard.

If you only knew the desperate loneliness of some of these missionaries, and the disastrous situations that can arise, born out of sheer loneliness, when nobody seems to care! They begin to look around for affection, for care, for interest, and find none: if then some serious crisis arises for their mind, their heart, whose fault is it? Theirs? No, yours and mine! There has been no evidence of interest, such as *the existence of a letter* might have provided.

As I pondered Paul's conclusion I was reminded again of

(ii) *The expression of the love*

We come back to this. That is why this church was such a lovely church. 'All the saints salute you.' 'Salute every saint in Christ.' All at Rome were interested in all at Philippi. Is your little church fellowship interested in any other fellowship, or are you all wrapped up in yourselves? As we leave Philippians let us not forget that we have found in it, amid so much else, *the expression of a love*.

And also

(iii) *The exaltation of the Lord*

I would like to note, as we close, how this
letter ends. 'Now unto God and our Father be
glory for ever and ever.' Could you end your
letters with that? Do you ever write a letter of
such a kind that you just could *not* write that at
the end of it? Then if you cannot write that at
the end, do not send the letter. Businessman,
could you write, 'Now unto God and our Father
be glory'? You have just tied up a deal. Can you
lift that letter, telling of that deal, up to God
and say, 'And now unto God our Father be
glory.'

That fellow, writing to that girl, what are you
writing about? Love is coming into your hearts
and you are facing all the tensions of that
difficult time. What is in your letter? Can you
take it and lift it up before God and say, 'And
now – and now, Father, unto Thee be glory'? If
you are not exalting your Lord in your letter, do
not send it.

That letter you are writing to someone at
home about another who is working on your
mission station, and writing out of the bitterness
of a difficult situation: can you take that letter
and at the end lift it up to God and say, 'And
now, Father, here is the letter. Unto thee – unto
thee – be glory'?

As our study of the Epistle of Joy draws to an
end, it is clear that a life of continual
rejoicing is most certainly offered to us in
Christ, whatever the place we are in, whoever
the people we are with, and even whatever the

kind of persons we *now* are. But there are
conditions. The story of the Philippian church
well illustrates how much a truly loving
fellowship with other Christians contributes to
our joy. The difficulties of our situation will call
for a truly Christian reaction that turns
opposition into opportunity, and deliberately
looks for the blessings that can surprise us. A
genuine care to maintain truly Christian
relationships is an essential factor in a happy
Christian life and witness. And so is the frank
recognition of our own spiritual poverty, which
only an abiding intimacy with Christ and
expectancy of joy can remove.

Paul has shown that there can be no joy
unless known wrongs are put right, and a mood
of genuine and unfailing gratitude is allowed to
breed a deep contentment. Through all else, the
cultivation of the life of prayer, mingled always
with praise, must keep our spiritual experience
ever new, ever fresh, ever close to our living and
triumphant Lord.

If we are ever to attain that quality of living,
that level of loving, that daily life 'sustained by
joy', we must end our study where Paul ends his
epistle, with the prayer for grace –

'The grace of our Lord Jesus Christ be with
you all. Amen.'